G

The
Buffalo
King

The Buffalo King

BY NANCY VEGLAHN

The Story of Scotty Philip

ILLUSTRATED BY DONALD CARRICK

CHARLES SCRIBNER'S SONS

NEW YORK

Printed in the United States of America
SBN 684-12492-0
Library of Congress Catalog Card Number 79-161470

**For
Ruth
Ann** A YOUNG SOUTH DAKOTAN

Author's Note

This story is based on the life of James "Scotty" Philip. The events described are taken from historical fact; conversations were created with every attempt to be true to the information known about the real-life characters in the book.

Scotty Philip did not singlehandedly save the American bison from extinction, but if it had not been for him and a few others like him these animals would undoubtedly have been wiped out. Although he was one of the most successful cattle ranchers of his time, it is as the "Buffalo King" that he is particularly remembered. The herd of purebred bison now living in Custer State Park in the Black Hills of South Dakota is descended from the Philip buffalo herd.

Contents

The buffalo are walking,
Over the whole earth they are walking.
The people are coming home,
The people are coming home,
Says my father, says my father.

Dakota Indian "Ghost Dance" song

Prologue Jamie Philip liked to win, and he usually did. It was Saint Andrew's Day, November 30, and the school in the little village of Dallas, Morayshire, Scotland, had been dismissed for the holiday. Bagpipes wailed, kilted men danced on the green, and boys spent the day competing in all the athletic contests that were popular in the 1860's.

Tired of conventional footraces, the boys decided to have a race with all the contestants blindfolded. They lined up, twitching like racehorses. Each had a large handkerchief tied over his eyes. Then someone yelled, "Go!"

The contestants blundered off in all directions, stumbling and laughing—all but Jamie Philip. Without hesitation the tall, black-haired boy loped to the finish alone.

"You could see!" accused one of his rivals.

"Aye, you must have moved the blindfold!" the others insisted.

"No," Jamie answered. "But I got the wind spotted."

All his life, James Philip had a knack for observing which way the wind was blowing. Later in life he was able to use that vision to make a name for himself as one of the most successful cattlemen in the United States. The same ability grieved him when the trends he saw were not so much to his liking.

In the valley of the Lossie River, part of the Scottish highlands, the land is rugged and wild. The tough, proud and independent people of that region were much like the men and women who settled the American west, and in fact many of the pioneers of America's last frontier were Scots.

James Philip was such a man. Growing up in Morayshire in the 1860's, he learned to rely on his own strength, and to be loyal to friends and family at the same time. Shrewdness was admired in the highlands; he learned to be foxy without being dishonest. Ambition and a hunger for adventure led him to dream of a new life in the land across the Atlantic Ocean.

Although his father had never traveled outside the Lossie valley, Jamie knew by the time he was in his teens that there was no future for him in Scotland. The little family farm could hardly support nine children once they married and started families of their own. Jamie's older brother, George, went to America first. In the spring of 1874 three more of the Philip boys followed him to settle in Kansas: Alex, David, and James.

1

Death on the Plains The first thing he noticed was the smell. Long before Jamie Philip saw the rotting buffalo carcasses, their stench poisoned the air with its message of decay and death. When the three riders finally paused at the top of a slope and looked out over a plain covered with hundreds of the huge corpses, Jamie's stomach lurched and he began to swallow rapidly.

"Phew!" said Tom Beverly, the guide Jamie and his brother Alex had hired to take them buffalo hunting, "Somebody done a lot of shooting here."

"But they didn't even take the meat," Alex said. "Why would anyone kill all these animals and just leave them?"

Tom shrugged. "Probably just took the tongues. That's what brings the best price now."

Jamie, still struggling to keep from losing his breakfast, said nothing. He shifted the heavy buffalo gun from one arm to the other and stared at the scene below. This had probably been a meadow not long before: there were still a few wildflowers to be seen, and the grass was lush between the bodies.

He felt cheated. Buffalo had thundered through his dreams ever since he had been old enough to read about America. Buffalo—

not the puny, ordinary creatures one saw in Scotland. Jamie had imagined himself matched against them, using every ounce of strength and wit he could muster just to stay alive. James Philip, the famous fur-trader; James Philip, Scout; James Philip, conqueror of the mighty buffalo . . .

Even as stinking carcasses, they were impressive. Jamie wondered who had killed them so casually and left them here to rot. He knew that the great herds were being exterminated; he had read it in the newspapers. That was why he and Alex had been in such a hurry to go looking for live buffalo, before it was too late. One article in a Kansas City paper had spoken of the "disappearance" of the animals. What a clean word that was, as though they had simply vanished in a puff of smoke.

"Maybe what I heard in Dodge City was right," Tom Beverly said. "Some of the fellows there told me that there won't be any buffalo hunting this year. Said they're gone, all dead. Sure is hard to believe."

They turned their horses and rode around the putrid field. Jamie's stomach settled. The warm summer sun felt good on his back, and he enjoyed the sweep of the western Kansas plains ahead. The guide entertained them with stories of his experiences as a buffalo hunter. He looked not much older than Jamie—perhaps twenty or so.

"Once I seen a herd of buffalo so big the sound of their hooves would deafen you," Tom told them. "After that herd went by I couldn't hear a thing for hours. There must have been ten thousand of 'em. We only shot a dozen or so. In those days we took everything: meat, hide and all. So you didn't kill any more than you had time to skin and cut up."

"How long ago was that?" Jamie asked.

"Three, four years ago."

"But if there were that many buffalo just a few years ago," Alex asked, "what happened to them? Why are there so few left?"

"Just too much hunting, I guess. You know, there's nothing much to killing buffalo. You'll find out if we come on some live ones."

It was late afternoon when Tom led them to a spot by the Smoky Hill River where the buffalo liked to drink. The place was a secluded hollow between two ridges, and Tom told the boys to dismount and tie their horses to a tree before they went over the first ridge.

Jamie crept up the ridge after Tom, with Alex following. When he got to the top, Tom turned with a grin and waved the other two up. Below them some fifteen buffalo were grazing peacefully beside the river.

Jamie held his breath. They were beautiful, with their massive heads, great shaggy humps and sleek bodies. The bulls were at least ten feet long and taller than a man. One of the animals glanced up and seemed to be looking directly at them.

"They'll see us!" Alex whispered.

"No," Tom told him, "buffalo are nearly blind. What we have to watch out for is the wind—if they smell us they'll run." He pulled a few blades of dry grass and tossed them into the air. "It's all right, the breeze is toward us."

Jamie felt the gun pressing hard and cold against his side. He had always liked to hunt. In Scotland he had often killed deer, pheasants, and grouse, and brought the meat home proudly. But this was different.

"Aim for the heart," Tom whispered. "It's just behind the shoulder blade, about two-thirds of the way down from the top of the hump. Come on."

Jamie and Alex followed Tom part way down the ridge, then stopped where he motioned and shouldered their rifles. Jamie never took his eyes off the little group of buffalo nearest them. It seemed incredible that they would just stand there, unseeing, and let themselves be killed.

"Now," said Tom, and fired. One of the animals jumped and fell with blood streaming from its nostrils. The others looked up at the sound of the shot and milled around nervously, but they did not run.

Jamie hesitated, then squeezed the trigger, sighting down the barrel at a magnificent bull only a few hundred yards away. The gun kicked violently against his shoulder. He saw the buffalo start, lunge forward, and then crumple slowly in the dirt.

Alex had fired at almost the same instant. Jamie looked around and saw that his brother had only hit the animal in the leg. It stumbled, wheeled around and began to charge directly toward them.

"Look out!" yelled Tom, leaping out of the wounded bull's path. Jamie grabbed Alex's arm and pulled him into some bushes. The buffalo came on like something out of a nightmare—swollen with rage, its mouth open and its mane flying. Then it stopped, so close that Jamie could hear its labored breathing. At the same time there was another shot. The bull sank to the ground, twitched and died.

"They're running," Tom said, reloading his smoking gun. "If you want to get another one you'll have to hurry . . ."

The buffalo had finally followed the lead of a bull and were charging across the far ridge and away from the river. Jamie felt no urge to go after them. Alex still sat on the ground where he had fallen a few minutes earlier. He got slowly to his feet, looking at the dead buffalo.

"I'm sorry," Alex said softly. He looked pale and shaken. "I just missed. I guess I aimed too low."

Jamie watched him curiously. Alex was usually a very good shot, and he had done a lot of hunting back in Scotland.

"Well, if you're satisfied, we'd better get to work on these carcasses," Tom told them. "You still want to try to take some of the meat, and the hides too?"

"Yes," Jamie said.

"The horses can only carry so much. I'll show you how to strip the hides and get the choicest meat off, and we'll leave the rest."

Tom Beverly took a wicked-looking knife from his belt and slit one of the dead buffalo expertly from head to tail. As he worked, Jamie and Alex watched. They had both killed and skinned deer, but one of these animals was bigger than five Scottish deer.

Jamie went to work on the bull he had killed. Before he made the first cut, he ran his hand over the hump and down the shoulders, touching the swell of muscle and bone under the shaggy coat. It made him feel small by comparison. This was a strange sensation, because Jamie Philip stood a head taller than most of the boys and men he knew, and his shoulders were too wide for any of the ready-made jackets in the Victoria dry goods store.

In spite of its strength, the bull was dead. And it had been pitifully easy to kill. Slicing through the tough hide, Jamie decided that it was no great honor to add another heap of buffalo bones to those already littering the Kansas countryside.

By the time they had the hides cut off and wrapped around small haunches of buffalo meat, it was almost dark. Tom found a good place to camp just down the river, and they roasted the meat over an open fire.

They ate quietly, listening to the night noises and looking at the star-flooded sky. Jamie was still captivated by the long view of the American plains. In Dallas, his home village in Scotland, the sky was usually hidden by clouds or fog. Even on clear days much of it was blotted out by the hills around the village. Here there seemed to be no limit to the world at all—just endless sky and rolling land.

"How do you like buffalo steak?" Tom asked.

"It's good—tastes a lot like beef," said Alex.

Jamie examined the last bite of rich, dark meat. "I think it's even better than venison."

Tom nodded. "Sure fed a lot of men on the railroad construction crews," he said. "When they were building the Kansas Pacific, the men had buffalo meat for breakfast, lunch and supper. That's how Buffalo Bill got his start."

"Is that why there's so few live buffalo left in Kansas?" Alex asked.

"That's part of the reason. But then after the railroads were finished they used to take people out hunting on the trains. Easterners would come out here and never even get off the passenger cars—just shoot as many buffalo as they could from the train windows."

Early the next morning the three men set out for home, with the raw hides slung across the backs of their horses. Three times during the day they passed fields of dead buffalo, some still rotting, some heaps of clean white bone. When they reached Hays City, Jamie and Alex paid Tom Beverly and watched him ride into town in a cloud of Kansas dust.

"What do you think, Jamie, was it worth ten dollars?" Alex asked, as they turned their horses toward Victoria.

"He earned it," Jamie said. "He's a good guide. But when I think it took me two months to save my half, and then all the trouble I went to borrowing that gun and knife and all . . ."

"It wasn't what we thought, was it?"

Buffalo hunters like this man left valleys of bones all over the West.

Jamie shook his head. "Killing them with these big guns is just too easy. And all those bones!"

"I think that's why I almost got us trampled," Alex said. "I'm not making excuses for my poor shooting, but when I looked at those animals just standing there it seemed like murder or something. At the last minute I let the gun slip, I didn't mean to shoot at all."

"Well, we got our baffalo robes," Jamie said. "I suppose George'll make us work twice as hard tomorrow to make up for what we missed today."

Alex groaned.

Jamie was glad to see Victoria Manor that evening. The Manor, a large stone building, served as a train depot, post office, store and hotel. It was the one imposing landmark in an otherwise dreary setting. After only a little more than a year of existence, George Grant's Victoria Colony was still struggling to establish itself.

It had started with a great dream. Jamie remembered when his older brother had heard George Grant speak in Edinburgh of the Kansas plains just waiting for settlers. "I will people these prairies with the best blood of England and Scotland," he had promised grandly.

George Philip was station agent at Victoria. He and his wife, Jane, and his younger brothers lived in rooms on the second floor of the Manor. George was also trying to farm some land nearby, and had imported cattle grazing on pastureland. It was there, on George's farmland, that Alex, David and Jamie Philip had done most of their work.

When they arrived, the three brothers had found that life in Victoria Colony was no lark. George was a hardworking man and he expected a great deal from his teenaged brothers. They rose with the sun, worked until dark, then fell exhausted into bed. There was no time for amusement, and the "town" of Victoria had little to offer in that line anyway.

Alex was the least rebellious of the three boys. He was quiet and serious and really seemed to enjoy the work with crops and animals. David hated everything about Victoria from the time they first arrived. A few days before the buffalo hunting trip he had simply disappeared, leaving a note saying that he was going to Canada.

As for Jamie, he veered between one extreme and the other. Sometimes he was so tired and angry he wanted to get on a horse and ride away, without money or even a destination in mind. He felt this way especially after long sessions in the fields. On the other hand, he liked working with the Aberdeen Angus cattle George had imported from Scotland. At such times, when he was allowed to tend the cattle, Jamie was almost contented. If only there were more to do around Victoria! He missed the sports and the parties in his home village; people at the colony seemed to think only of work.

Bone-tired as he was when he rode into town that evening, Jamie knew that he would have to be in the wheat field at sunrise. He and Alex stabled the horses, brushed the worst of the dust from their clothes, then went into the Manor.

The thick stone walls kept it quite cool inside, even in August. Jamie wandered through the store, looking idly at too-small jackets and leather boots, while Alex bought several newspapers.

"Got the Kansas City *Star,* the New York *Herald* and even *Harper's Weekly,*" Alex reported when he found Jamie buying a small bag of licorice.

"Let's look at them for a minute before we go up," Jamie suggested. Reading the papers was a sort of entertainment, and also one of the few links they had with the outside world.

They sat in the chairs provided for patrons along one wall of the building. Alex read the *Star,* and Jamie thumbed through the pages of *Harper's Weekly.*

He was still bewildered by the American political system, and he glanced only briefly at stories of the coming Congressional elections and the scandals in Grant's administration. There were articles on new inventions and plays on the New York stage, and advertisements for hundreds of products. He savored the words and their tales of other places, triumphs and disasters, inventions, battles, celebrations, crimes. In spite of the fact that he had never been known as a "scholar," reading was one of Jamie's deepest pleasures. The schoolmaster at Dallas had despaired of teaching Jamie Philip anything else, once he learned to read. And Jamie would read almost anything—as long as no one told him he had to.

There was an article about the buffalo hunts and about efforts to pass a law protecting the animals. Such a law had actually been passed once, but President Grant had never signed it. One politician was quoted complaining about the way buffalo impeded progress: "They eat the grass. They trample upon the plains. They are as uncivilized as the Indian."

The words prickled Jamie. "Get out of my way," he translated. There was a sort of rudeness about the whole attitude that bothered him. Well, he had killed one too; maybe he should not feel so self-righteous about it. He turned the page.

Then Jamie saw the full-page story and forgot about everything else. "Alex," he almost shouted, "look at this. That expedition Custer took into the Black Hills this summer, they found gold!"

"Yes, there's something in the *Star* about it too," Alex said calmly.

"But that's not very far from here." Jamie's words ran together and tripped over each other. "We could go and make a fortune; no more farming, no more working for George . . ."

Alex laughed. "That's the quickest fortune anybody ever made. The Black Hills aren't all that close—all the way across Nebraska and up into Dakota Territory. Anyway, that's Indian country."

"It says here that the government is going to try to make a new treaty with the Sioux, so the gold in the Hills can be mined."

"Aye, but that will take time. Right now we'd best get to bed. You can wait at least 'til tomorrow to dig up your fortune."

2

Porcupine Meat One morning just four months later, Jamie rode into the Black Hills with three other young men he had met in Cheyenne, Wyoming Territory, the closest town to the gold fields. He had left a year of his life behind at Victoria Manor. All his possessions were rolled up in a blanket tied behind his saddle. He even had a new name.

"Scotch, ain't you?" Boston Smith had asked him that first night when they had met in the hotel lobby in Cheyenne. "Never heard anybody but the Scotch roll their r's like that."

"Yes," Jamie had said, "I'm from Scotland—or I was. I'm an American now."

"Well, Scotty, you look like you could do your share of the diggin'. How about going up to the Hills with us next week?"

So he had joined Boston Smith, Hi Kelly and Ike Humphrey in getting supplies and planning the prospecting trip. And from that time on the name "Scotty" stuck, even in his own mind. Jamie sounded juvenile, James was too formal—Scotty Philip seemed to suit him perfectly.

Now the four of them saw a bustling little settlement ahead in the valley. A group of men had been here for several weeks—illegally, for a treaty had not yet been signed with the Sioux. They had named the mining camp "Custer," after the famous Indian fighter. Some of the men were even plotting out streets, planning businesses they could establish with the money they earned from their gold discoveries. No one had found much gold as yet, just a nugget here and there, but they were all sure that as soon as they dug a little deeper and set up more efficient equipment for washing the gravel, they would be rich men.

"I hear they're planning a regular town here," Boston said, peering nearsightedly down the trail. "Maybe we can get a good piece of land, if the soldiers don't break things up."

Ike Humphrey yawned, stretching his long, thin face grotesquely. "It's not as if there was some good reason for kicking us out," he said. "Treaty's just a piece of paper. What do those Indians want with the Black Hills, anyway?"

"Gold don't mean anything to them," Hi Kelly agreed. "Now, when I get *my* share, I'll know what to do with it. How about you, Scotty? You Scotch are supposed to be pretty sharp with a dollar. How you going to spend yours?"

"I might invest in cattle," Scotty said. "Then again, I'd like to travel around the world, or build a railroad; I don't want to stay in one place for too long . . ."

The dreaming was wonderful. Scotty felt like a young king, riding into the mining settlement with his new friends. Now it was all worth while: the arguments with George, until he finally agreed to let Scotty come to Dakota Territory; the disappointment when Alex refused to join him; the long, lonely miles he had traveled on horseback; the cold food and rain and bugs.

They made camp and spent the rest of the day looking around, talking with the other prospectors and searching for a piece of land that had not already been claimed.

The next day they settled on a claim just north of the "town." There was a good water supply in a streamlet that ran through their little gulch, and Boston said the rock looked like the kind that often contained gold. Boston had spent more time in Cheyenne than the other three, and he had seen the minerals brought down out of the hills by earlier prospectors who had been ejected by the army.

They soon began digging. It was hard work, much harder than Scotty had imagined. And in the first few days they did not find even the slightest trace of "color" in the gray rocks and dirt. They decided to split up and cover more ground. Ike and Hi camped and worked at the low end of the gulch, near the main settlement. Boston and Scotty worked farther up in the hills. Still they turned up nothing promising.

It all ended one morning late in October. Scotty and Boston were climbing the steep side of a hill up the gulch, looking for new diggings. Scotty was not conscious of any sound except the crunching of golden leaves beneath his feet. Suddenly he heard shouts and turned to see a line of blue-coated soldiers riding into Custer.

"Get down," he called to Boston. "It's the army!"

They watched as their fellow prospectors packed under the eyes of the soldiers.

"I'm not leaving," Boston whispered angrily. "Not until I find some gold, anyway. Let's bring our horses up here—we've got to have them."

"You think the others will tell the soldiers about us?" Scotty asked.

"Ike and Hi wouldn't. In all that confusion, I'll bet nobody else will even miss us. Most of our stuff is up here on our claim. The soldiers won't look this far. Come on."

It was easy enough for Scotty and Boston to slip back down to the claim, get their horses and what gear they could carry, and move back up the hill to a sheltered gully. No one came to look for them. Early in the afternoon, they saw the soldiers and the banished prospectors ride out of the camp and down the trail toward Cheyenne.

"We've got it all to ourselves, partner," Boston grinned happily. "They won't come back here for months—probably not until spring. By then we could be rich!"

Scotty nodded, realizing suddenly that the two of them were the only men in the camp, probably the only men in the vast mountain area known as the Black Hills, unless . . .

"What about Indians?" he asked softly.

"Oh, they won't bother us." Boston's expression lost a little of its delight. "Tell you what, though, maybe we ought to sleep up here. That main camp's a little exposed. We could build a fire right there at the mouth of the gully to scare animals off."

"If there were Indians around they'd see the fire," Scotty pointed out.

"We'll keep it small and take turns sleeping and standing watch."

"We can't stay here all winter, Boston. We don't have the supplies, or a good enough shelter, and with just the two of us here we'd never survive anyway. Remember, we thought the army was going to open up the Black Hills for prospecting, and there'd be regular freighting in from Cheyenne."

"Oh, all right." Boston sounded irritated at Scotty's objections. "We'll go back by December at the latest. We can still do a lot of digging before then—if you're not afraid to stay."

"Did I say I was afraid?" Scotty glared at Boston, his muscles tense. He had rarely fought with anyone; there seemed to be no point in it since he was so much bigger and stronger than most men. But now he was really angry; he wanted to hit Boston, and something in the back of his mind told him that his friend was right. He was afraid.

In the face of Scotty's anger, Boston backed down quickly.

"I'm sorry, I didn't mean that," he said. "Just hadn't thought of all those things. Well, anyway, we can work for a few weeks. No telling what we'll find, right?"

"Right . . . no telling."

The same afternoon they found some tantalizing specks of gold or "color" in the gravel near the streamlet, and they began serious digging. At night, they slept in the gully. At first they took turns keeping watch for Indians, but they were both exhausted after the day's digging and found it hard to stay awake. When a week passed without trouble they gave up the constant watching. Each of them would simply check the fire and the camp if he happened to wake during the night.

Scotty was still uneasy. Distant noises startled him. Sometimes he caught a flicker of movement in the corner of his eye, off in the woods, and he would wonder. In the evening, he would hunt for fresh meat to add to their dwindling food supply. Once he saw some oddly broken branches, with no trace of animal tracks.

Late one night Boston shook Scotty awake roughly. "The horses," he said, "they're gone!"

Scotty scrambled up and followed Boston to the place where their horses had been hobbled. As Boston had said, they were gone. The pale moonlight revealed no sign of them, except for a slight disturbance of the leaves and pine needles.

"What . . . ?"

"Shhh." Boston cut off Scotty's question sharply. Then he whispered, "Listen."

Far in the distance, Scotty heard a muffled sound that might have been made by horses' hooves.

"Thievin' Indians," Boston growled. "We better follow now, or we'll never get those horses back."

If we don't, Scotty thought, we'll never get back to Cheyenne. They crept after the faint sounds for what seemed like many miles. The Indians were following the bank of a dry creek bed which wound down and out of the hills. At least, Scotty thought, they might be able to find their way back to camp later. He had his rifle in one hand and a knife in his boot, but he wondered how much help they would be against a band of horse-stealing Indians.

They came out of the foothills and onto a stretch of prairie-like land at the edge of the Black Hills. It was not so easy to stay out of sight now, and they had to creep along behind, following the faint sounds of the horses.

Boston saw the Indian camp first and put up a hand to stop Scotty. They both dropped down in the tall grass and crawled on their bellies to a rise overlooking the circled tepees.

Scotty peered through the grass, intensely curious in spite of the tension in his body. He had never seen a "wild" Indian before. A few men were moving about the camp, and he could hear them talking in deep, gutteral voices. Once, three or four of them laughed loudly together. In that moment they sounded like a group of men sharing a joke on a street corner in Edinburgh or Victoria.

The men disappeared into their various tepees, and finally the camp seemed to be quiet except for a few dogs roaming around. Dawn was near; the bright moonlight in which they had been traveling faded into a sort of early-morning gray. Boston pointed to the left of the village, where the Indian ponies were standing, and crawled off that way through the grass.

Scotty followed. He could see his pinto hobbled at the edge of the group of horses, so he worked his way toward it. Boston was going in the opposite direction; he had apparently spotted his horse, too.

Now Scotty could think of nothing but untying his horse and getting away as quickly as possible. He got on his hands and knees, and started to run in a crouching position. He was almost to the pinto when he tripped over something and landed flat in the spiky grass.

He rolled over and found himself lying next to a young Indian whose face was not more than a foot from his own. For an instant they stared at each other with blank surprise. The Indian looked about the same age as Scotty, and his face was framed by long braids wrapped in some kind of cloth or fur. He reached out and grabbed Scotty, calling out in a loud voice, *"Wasichu! Wasichu!"*

Scotty got to his feet and shook himself loose from the Indian's grasp. He ran for the pinto, untied it, jumped on and rode away bareback as fast as he could go. He could hear shouts and the sound of gunshots behind him.

He rode wildly, both he and the pinto breathing with labored gasps, hurtling along the creek bed. All the way, Scotty looked and listened for Boston, but he saw no sign of his friend.

Scotty slowed down when he got into the high hills again. He could hear no sound of pursuit now. He considered going back to the claim but decided against it. The Indians knew where that camp was. If they wanted the pinto—or its owner—badly enough they might come there again. He decided to move south through the hills in the direction of Cheyenne.

But where was Boston? Riding slowly through the dark, with branches whipping against his face, Scotty listened until his head ached. There was nothing but the usual night noises. There seemed to be little doubt about it: Boston Smith had been captured by the Sioux.

It wasn't my fault, Scotty told himself. I didn't see that guard until I fell over him. It wasn't my fault.

Stories of Indian atrocities came to life in his imagination; he saw his friend tortured, scalped, burned at the stake. Worst of all, he could not resist the feeling that he was glad it was Boston who had been captured, and not him.

As the sun rose above the highest peaks he stopped to drink at a creek. After washing his face in the icy water, he sat down on a rock to try to think things through. There was nothing he could do for Boston Smith now; he would have to try to get out of the wilderness himself. He had lost his gun in the scuffle at the Indian camp. Luckily there was a spare blanket rolled up and tied across his horse's back, so he could probably keep warm enough. He had no food at all, and only the knife for hunting.

Yet somehow his panic and fear faded in the sunlight. He had always loved to be alone in a wild place, to feel a part of the teeming life around him. These hills were not low and bare like the hills of his village in Scotland. They were rugged, tree-covered, pulling his eyes upward to their granite peaks. Someone had told him that the Indians believed their gods lived in these mountains. He could see why they might think so.

All day Scotty rode through the hills, finding trails when he could and pushing his way through the underbrush when there were no trails. He saw a deer once, and later a wild turkey, but with only a knife for a weapon he could not hope to catch and kill them.

By nightfall he was famished. He looked for berries but saw nothing that looked edible. Finally he made camp near another creek and spent an hour trying vainly to catch a fish. He went to sleep with his stomach growling and aching.

In the morning Scotty climbed a tall spruce tree to see whether he could spot a good trail out of the hills. About forty feet up the tree he met a porcupine on its way down.

It was larger than he would have expected. Scotty drew back instinctively, trying to remember whether porcupines could actually shoot their quills or whether they just hit attackers with their tails. The animal stared at Scotty with a rather bored expression and moved around to the other side of the tree.

Meat! Could you eat a porcupine?

Scotty broke off a branch, reached out carefully and swung it at the porcupine. The animal hung on for a moment and then fell. Scotty clamored eagerly down the tree, but by the time he got to the bottom the porcupine had rolled to its feet and was walking away.

Desperately, Scotty looked for a weapon. The knife was no good with those sharp quills. He picked up the heaviest rock he could see and hurled it with all his strength. At last, the porcupine lay still on the ground.

By the time Scotty had skinned and cleaned the little animal, there was almost nothing left. The quills had made it look much larger than it actually was. He built a fire and roasted the tiny pieces of meat on a stick.

Hungry as he was, he could barely force himself to eat it. The meat was so tough it was almost impossible to chew. It had a revolting, salty taste. Afterwards he drank great quantities of creek water and told himself that at least he had something in his stomach.

I may be hungry again, he thought as he rode away, but I hope I'm never hungry enough to eat porcupine meat.

3

Scotty Philip, Scout Scotty struggled into the crowded restaurant next to the Ford Hotel in Cheyenne, ordered steak and eggs, and began to eat. Nothing had ever tasted so good.

"Philip! Did those bluecoats chase you out, too?" Ike Humphrey pushed through the crowd to Scotty's table, his bony face creased with a big smile.

"Not soldiers—Indians," Scotty said between bites.

"Ah, we wondered if you'd have trouble with them. Where's Boston?"

Scotty shook his head, and his pleasure in the meal faded. "I don't know. Maybe the Indians got him. They took our horses, and we went to get them back. We got separated, and I haven't seen him since."

"Too bad. Some of the stories you hear about what those savages do to prisoners . . . Well, hope he got away safe. You going back home this winter?"

"No, not if I can find work around here."

"Why don't you sign on as an army scout? Sounds like there might be some action against the Indians. That's what I'd do, except my brother needs some help at our place in Montana."

"You think they'd hire me?" Scotty asked. "I haven't got any experience scouting, and I don't know this part of the country too well yet."

"Ahh, you've got a good sense of direction, you could find your way most anyplace." Ike grinned. "Besides, you *look* like a dangerous man. We know you're a peaceful sort, but the army doesn't. And they like their scouts to look mean and tough."

"Maybe I should grow my hair long, like Custer, or get a fancy rig like Buffalo Bill wears."

"Wouldn't hurt! Well, Scotty, maybe I'll see you here next spring . . ."

Scotty stayed on in Cheyenne until late November, doing whatever odd jobs he could find. But there were too many unemployed men in town, most of them surly and spoiling for fights, and there was not nearly enough work to go around.

One cold, clear morning Scotty picked up a newspaper in the lobby of the Ford Hotel and read the headline:

SIOUX ORDERED BACK TO RESERVATIONS

Those Not Returned By Jan. 31
To Be Declared Hostiles;
Army Action Likely Soon

And farther down in the story, the note everyone was looking for: "Black Hills to be opened to prospectors? ? ?"

Scotty knew from the gossip he had heard around town that many Indians had been given permission to leave their agencies and go buffalo hunting in the Powder River country, north of the Black Hills. Now they were to be brought back in the middle of the winter, and those who did not come voluntarily would be considered "hostile" even if they sat peacefully in their winter camps. The whole thing sounded like a convenient excuse to declare the Treaty of 1868 void and take the Black Hills.

It was too bad, Scotty thought, that the thing could not have been negotiated and had to be worked out in such an under-handed way. But then, it was none of his affair.

Scotty rode over to Fort Fetterman early in December. He was completely out of funds, and Ike's idea of scouting for the army seemed to be his only chance to hang on until spring. A guard at Fort Fetterman directed him to the post quartermaster, a red-faced little man with a wispy blonde beard.

"Any experience?" the quartermaster asked in a squeaky voice.

"Not with the army. But I'm a good horseman, and I've worked with cattle a lot, and I've traveled—north of Cheyenne." Scotty had almost mentioned his trip to the Black Hills, but decided that might not be a good idea.

"Indians?"

"I tracked down an Indian camp once, got back a horse they had stolen from me, and escaped."

The quartermaster nodded, and looked him over as though he were a horse for sale. "Well, you're a big one, ain't you?" he muttered. "Indians are impressed by a big man. We might be able to use you to carry dispatches. Sixty dollars a month, and we hire you a month at a time. That all right?"

"Yes, fine."

"I'll show you where you can sleep. There's one end of the barracks we keep for scouts, and we've got a bunk free now. Come along."

Life at Fort Fetterman was incredibly dull. In the next three weeks Scotty had only one assignment: he carried a dispatch from Fort Fetterman to a small troop of soldiers on the edge of the Black Hills. The rest of the time he spent taking care of the horses, reading whatever books and newspapers he could find, and playing cards with other bored soldiers and scouts.

General George Crook had his headquarters at the Fort. The famous Indian fighter was almost as tall as Scotty, and looked very impressive in his dress uniform. His beard parted naturally in the middle. On windy days he appeared with the beard braided, to keep it from flapping and getting tangled in the wind.

Scotty tried growing a beard several times that winter, but he always gave up and shaved it off after a few weeks of itching and trimming. He finally left a moustache. By the end of January he was so used to it that it felt as much a part of his face as his nose or his chin.

The January 31 deadline passed, but according to the newspapers only a few small bands of Sioux returned to their reservations. Rumors circulated around the Fort: there were more than a thousand "hostile" Indians camped in the Powder River country; the army was going to move out; there would be fighting at last.

When General Crook left Fort Fetterman with twelve companies of soldiers March 1, 1876, Scotty went with them. The first few days of the march up the old Bozeman Trail in Wyoming Territory were pleasant. The sun was warm, the snow and ice began to melt, and the breeze was mild. Scotty chatted with his friends, who ranged from the cook's ancient assistant to Lieutenant Sibley of General Crook's staff. Sibley was a young officer Scotty especially liked. They had spent long hours during the winter arguing politics and exchanging stories.

Early one morning, the temperature started to drop rapidly. The wind turned cold, and the air was soon filled with snow. Scotty stumbled along, his face stung by the blizzard, trying to get the horses to shelter and keep them supplied with food.

The whole company waited a day for the storm to let up, but there was no improvement. Some of the men became sick. All of them were cold and discouraged. The thermometers would not even register, so they knew it was more than thirty-eight degrees below zero.

Crook moved them out after two days, leaving most of the supply wagons behind with a small force of soldiers and the sick. One of the regular scouts was among those too ill to move on, so Scotty was sent in his place.

Crook divided his column in order to cover more ground in the search for the Sioux. Early the second day, the three companies that Scotty and Lieutenant Sibley were with found tracks of Indian ponies along the Powder River.

Though it was still bitterly cold, the air had finally cleared. It was not difficult to follow the tracks back among the bluffs beside the river. Moving as quietly as they could, the soldiers traced them through the drifts.

Just after dawn they stopped at the top of a high bluff and saw the Indian village below. Scotty stood beside Sibley and stared down at the shadowy circle of tepees. This was a larger village than the one he and Boston had found. There was no one stirring.

"Looks to me like Cheyennes, from the markings on the tepees," Sibley whispered.

"What do we do now?" asked Scotty.

"That's up to Reynolds." Colonel Reynolds, who was senior officer in the three companies that had followed the pony tracks, came toward them with his two aides.

"Attack when you hear the signal," one of the aides told them.

"Attack?" Sibley grabbed the man by one arm. "Who's down there? How do we know they're hostile?"

Reynolds heard him and rushed over, pushing his face close to Sibley's. "Any Indians we find in this territory are to be considered hostile," he hissed. "We'll burn the village, take their horses, anything we have to do to convince them to go back to the reservation."

"What if they were on their way back?" Sibley asked.

"They should have started sooner."

Scotty stood listening uneasily to the exchange. Lieutenant

Sibley was his friend; but Reynolds had the authority. Scotty would simply have to take orders—something he did not like to do.

The orders came a few moments later, with a sounding bugle and a cavalry charge down the hill. It was like something out of a storybook, like the great battles he had read about as a child— until they reached the village.

Scotty reined up and saw a woman coming out of the first tepee, her eyes wide and frightened. Behind her was a small child, still rubbing the sleep from his eyes. Scotty stared at them, unsure as to what he was supposed to do. Was this the enemy? A soldier raced up from behind, waving a lighted torch. He thrust it against the tepee, and the woman grabbed up the child and ran away.

Rifles cracked; shouts and screams chorused with the wailing of the cold wind. Scotty decided to go for the horses tethered at the end of the camp. He raced through the village, swerving to avoid trampling the people who ran before him.

Five or six Indian men reached the ponies first. Driving most of the animals ahead of them, the warriors rode off toward the hills. Scotty managed to cut off a half dozen ponies and started back toward the bluff with them.

The village was in flames. Scotty could see bodies among the burning tepees. He stopped at a distance and got the ponies tied together, using his lariat as a lead rope. He was just mounting his horse again when Lieutenant Sibley came toward him, leading a group of children and an old man away from the deadly crossfire in the village.

Sibley's handsome face sagged; he looked ten years older. "This is Two Moons' camp," he called in a strange, harsh voice.

"Who's Two Moons?" Scotty asked.

"A friendly Cheyenne. At least he *was* friendly."

Scotty rubbed a hand over his face, feeling the sharp stubble of two days' whiskers. "I don't understand what's going on. Why are we fighting these people?"

"You heard the officer. Any Indian in this area is hostile. Even this old man, these children. Burn the village, take the horses. And if they have the impudence to resist—"

"Looks like that's what they're going to do." Scotty pointed to the high bluff from which the soldiers had first spotted the camp. The sun was climbing, and its harsh light outlined dozens of warriors, firing down from the bluff at the bluecoats.

"How'd they get up there?" a soldier yelled from the edge of the burning village.

"I'm hit!" another cried, clutching his leg.

They milled around in confusion for a few minutes, and then Scotty heard the bugler sounding retreat. He fell in with the others, still leading the string of ponies.

At first the retreat was orderly enough. But the Indians saw that their enemies were going and swept down from the bluff after them. The retreat became a panic.

Scotty could not keep up with the racing cavalrymen. Looking back at the pursuers, he decided it would be impossible to get away with a string of Indian ponies. He let go of the lead rope and galloped away as fast as his pinto would take him.

The Cheyenne warriors followed them for the rest of the day, never quite catching up but making their presence known whenever the soldiers tried to stop and rest. Scotty was too hungry, cold, and exhausted to think about what the day had meant. Near sunset, he looked around and saw no sign of the Cheyennes. Still he urged his mount forward.

They reached the main column that night. Scotty saw the surprise on the faces of the rest of Crook's soldiers as the bedraggled cavalrymen trailed into camp. He had a fleeting memory of headlines in the Kansas papers just a year ago, when he had been a boy marveling over the exploits of the bluecoated Indian fighters: "Army Whips Sioux"; "Kiowas Humbled as Red River War Ends"; "White Captives Delivered from Cheyenne Camp."

Dirty and hungry as he was, he rolled up in his blanket and slept.

4

Gravel "Custer'll have those Sioux back on the reser-
and Gold vation in a week! Either that, or dead."

"I heard there was three columns on the way to the Powder
River Country: Custer, Terry, and Crook."

"The Seventh Cavalry could handle a few hundred mangy Indians by itself. Everybody knows one of Custer's men is worth at
least ten Sioux."

Scotty Philip did not join in the optimistic talk along the main
street of the new town of Custer. It was early June, 1876, and he
had been in the Black Hills for nearly a month. This time the soldiers were out pursuing Indians instead of moving gold-hunters
out of the Hills. There was a war on.

Memories of that morning in the Indian camp gave Scotty a
different viewpoint from that of most of the prospectors. He was
not so sure of the superiority of the Army in fighting "savages."
But he said nothing because he was not particularly proud of his
own performance that day.

The army had not looked with great favor on Colonel Reynolds' attack on the Two Moons village either. In fact, the Colonel had been court-martialed. Scotty had been back in Cheyenne
at that time, but he had read about it in the newspapers. The

strange thing was that no one seemed concerned about the wisdom of charging in on a sleeping camp of friendly Indians; what *had* upset Reynolds' superiors was the fact that a retreat had been ordered so quickly. It was even suggested that Reynolds had left a wounded soldier to fall into the hands of the Indians.

Now the United States Army was sending more than a thousand men out to meet the Sioux. No one was sure how many Indians they would find, but the men Scotty talked to in Custer were positive of one thing. The Indian problem would be solved once and for all. And then the prospectors could finally get on with the business of making their fortunes.

So far, that business was not going particularly well for Scotty. He and his two friends, Ike Humphrey and Hi Kelly, had built a green-timber shack to live in and had begun to work their claim again. They found some gold, but only enough to pay their expenses and keep them hoping. Boston Smith did not turn up in Cheyenne or in Custer, though Scotty kept looking for him.

One hot and muggy day, Scotty walked back to the claim from the store, where he had gone to buy flour and other supplies. He found Ike and Hi shoveling gravel into the rocker they had bought from a discouraged miner who had gone home. They were glad to stop work for a few minutes and get the news from town.

"Everyone thinks there'll be action against the Indians soon," Scotty reported.

"About time," said Ike. "I hope they sent a strong force up there. The Sioux are good fighters."

"Not according to what I heard in town. Most of the men there figure Custer could lick the Sioux with the Seventh Cavalry alone."

Hi wiped the sweat off his broad forehead with a rag. "Greenhorns might think that," he said, "or kids that've read too many dime novels. Anybody that's lived in the West for long knows you don't fool around with the Sioux. And they'd love to have that long, yellow hair of Custer's."

"Oh, that's another thing," said Scotty. "Somebody told me Custer cut his hair."

Ike grinned. "I think Colonel Custer has dreams of going into politics—maybe even running for President. And who'd vote for a President with long hair?"

"He'll have to beat the Sioux first," said Hi.

They went back to work. Scotty picked up a shovel and scooped gravel into the rocker, while Ike poured creek water through it and Hi rocked it back and forth. The rocker looked something like a cradle. In the bottom of it was a piece of sheet-iron punched full of holes. The gold dust was supposed to be washed down through these holes and caught on the cleats in the bottom of the rocker, while the larger gravel stayed in the top.

The machine worked fairly well. But it required a fantastic amount of labor to "wash" a very small amount of gold. They had to work the rocker on the banks of Custer Creek in order to use the available water. Gravel from their diggings at the base of a hill had to be carried in fifty-pound flour sacks and then shoveled into the rocker.

They tried to share the work fairly, but Scotty was so much stronger than the other two that he usually volunteered to do the carrying. One sack of gravel was not much of a burden on his broad shoulders. However, by the end of the day he was sore and exhausted.

After a month they figured that they had earned a little more than a hundred dollars apiece. It was not too bad; some of the men they knew had not even made enough to buy food and supplies. Others, a very few, had become rich men.

Scotty had to admit to himself that if his brother George had

made him work this hard, he would have felt like a slave. They kept at it even on Sundays. The first full day they took without doing any work at all was the Fourth of July, when they went to the celebration in Custer of the one hundredth birthday of the United States of America.

On an evening two weeks later they sat talking with a group of other miners outside the General Store. There were some old kegs and barrels to sit on, and it was a good spot from which to watch the activity on Main Street.

The talk was all of the big strike at Deadwood Gulch. Many of the men who had been working around Custer had already gone north to try their luck at the new Deadwood camp. Some, like Scotty, argued that it was foolish to pull up stakes and start all over again when they had already begun working claims near Custer. Others were sure that the Deadwood area was much richer in gold.

In the middle of this discussion, they noticed the arrival of a stagecoach at the other end of the street. Almost immediately a crowd gathered around it. Scotty could hear the buzz of excited talk, and he wondered what news the stagecoach driver had brought. Then a man came running down the street, shouting:

"Custer's been killed! Custer's dead!"

Scotty and his friends looked at each other uncertainly for a moment, wondering if they had misunderstood. Then they jumped up and raced to join the crowd around the stagecoach. The driver stood answering questions, obviously enjoying his sudden importance.

"There was a battle somewhere near the Little Bighorn," he said. "The Seventh found an Indian camp, bigger than anybody thought it would be. There was a battle, and they killed Custer and all his men."

"Not the whole Seventh Cavalry?" someone asked.

"Every man. At least all that were with Custer. Terry came on the scene later and found 'em all dead."

There was a stunned silence on the crowded street. The unbelievable had happened. Instead of finishing off the Indians once and for all, the army had been beaten.

"Did Terry's troops get the Sioux then?" a man near Scotty called to the driver.

"No, they got away. Crook and Terry are going to go after them later, I heard."

Custer's sudden and incredible death left the town that bore his name, and every other white settlement in the Black Hills, in immediate danger. Men drifted back dejectedly to their camps, bunching together for mutual protection.

Scotty lay awake for hours. He listened to the night noises that he usually ignored: squirrels and chipmunks running over the roof of the shack, crickets, unidentifiable rustlings. He thought of Lieutenant Sibley and the other soldiers he had known at the Fort. They would be off in pursuit of the Sioux now, he supposed. And those other young men of the Seventh Cavalry— what had their last moments been like?

Scotty got up early the next morning and tried to write a letter "home" (to George and Jane in Kansas). He did not write often, because he never seemed to be able to get his feelings down on paper. Usually he would resort to filling the letter with lists of supplies he had bought, or descriptions of his travels and how many miles it was from one creek to another. He knew that this did not satisfy his anxious relatives, for they kept writing and asking how he was and, of course, when he would be coming back to Kansas.

He stared at the blank paper. What he wanted was to be able to write of some triumph, a fortune made or at least a modest stake. He wanted to show them that he had been right to come to

the Black Hills, that he could succeed on his own. But he could
think of nothing but bad news:

> We have begun to dig a drain 9 feet deep and are going to dig
> till we come to something or give it up, and if nothing here look
> out for a call for a little money. It will look funny to you as it does
> to others, but I have not 50 cents although it would save my life.

He considered mentioning the massacre of Custer's troops but
decided against it. They would hear about it, if they hadn't already, and it would only add to their worries about him. It was
time to start work; Scotty put the letter away, to be finished later,
and picked up his shovel.

Through the rest of the summer there were Indian raids in and
around the Hills. Miners slept with their guns close and never
ventured far from the populated areas. It was rumored that the
Lawrence County commissioners had offered a $250 bounty for
any Indian, dead or alive, killed or captured.

In September Ike and Hi went with a large group of prospectors to Deadwood to look over the available claims, while Scotty
stayed behind to guard the Custer diggings. They came back
without much hope of getting rich in Deadwood gulch.

"All the good claims were gone long ago," Ike told Scotty the
day they returned. "There must be ten thousand men in that
gulch, all digging like prairie dogs. Most of 'em are half starved
and broke, and with winter coming on too. I think we'd be better
off to spend the winter here, where we at least know we can
make a living."

"What news is there about Crook and the Indians?" Scotty
asked.

"Crook's camped by Bear Butte right now, just outside the
Hills," Ike said. "So I guess we can feel a little safer for a while.

He had one little fight with some of the Sioux, east of here at a place called Slim Buttes. But Crazy Horse and a lot of the others are still on the loose."

Ike and Hi had brought the Deadwood newspapers back for Scotty to read. That night he looked through them by the light of a lamp that balanced precariously on their one rickety table. He read, and then reread, an editorial in one of the back issues:

WHAT WE WANT

To the Black Hiller there is a question that more nearly concerns him than all the gold he may gather. Is he always to be in dread of the murderous red man? . . . You might as well try to raise a turkey from a snake egg as to raise a good citizen from a papoose. Indians can be made good only in one way and that is to make angels of them.

There was more of the same, all expressing the idea that the government ought to exterminate the Indians and give the Black Hills, and its gold, to the "noble white man."

Ike and Hi, tired from their trip, had already rolled up in their blankets. Scotty read the editorial aloud to them.

"So?" Hi asked sleepily.

"It just seemed strange to me, talking about the 'murderous' Indians and then in the same breath claiming we should kill them all off."

Ike peered at Scotty through half-closed eyes. "That's what most people think. Are you for trying to dress 'em up, educate 'em and make white men of 'em, like some of those Easterners say we should?"

"I don't know. It just seems to me they're human beings, after all. This was their land. The only reason we're after it now is because of the gold."

"Well, there's more of us than there are of them. They weren't doing anything with the gold. Anyway, it's not our problem—the government will have to figure it out." Ike rolled over and was soon snoring.

The three of them dug in for the winter. They bought supplies, patched the cracks in their cabin and chopped firewood. Time passed slowly after the snow clogged the trails. Scotty went hunting and set traps for beaver. He spent many hours trudging through the forest, checking his trap lines.

Shortly after Christmas, Scotty made up his mind that he had had enough of gold-hunting. When spring came, he was leaving. The claim had supported him for a summer, but that was all. He would never make the fortune he had dreamed of by shoveling Black Hills gravel.

In fact, the whole idea of digging for gold had lost its glamor. Scotty was tired of the ugliness of the gold camps set down like warts in the natural beauty of the mountains. He was tired of the back-breaking work and the foolish hopes.

"You going back to Kansas, then?" Ike asked when Scotty announced his decision.

"No. I'm not ready to go back there yet, not empty-handed. I thought I might try scouting again, or maybe get a job working with cattle. I'm good at that."

"Why don't you go down by Camp Robinson?" Hi suggested. "I heard there's a cattle outfit getting started there. And there's an army post, too, so you could do both."

"Robinson—that's in Nebraska somewhere, isn't it?" Scotty asked.

Ike pulled the knife from his belt and got down on his knees. He began drawing a crude map in the dirt floor of the claim shack. "Here's the Cheyenne River," he said, indicating a wiggly line he had made. "And down here's the border between Ne-

braska and Dakota Territory. Here in the southwest corner of
Nebraska is the White River, and Camp Robinson's right beside
it, about here."

"Isn't Red Cloud camped around there now?" Hi asked.

Ike nodded. "When we were in Deadwood we heard they
were setting up an agency there by Camp Robinson, and Red
Cloud and his Sioux had made winter camp near it. Somebody
said that's where they're taking all the Sioux and Cheyennes they
round up, even Crazy Horse—if they ever catch him."

Spring was late that year, but as soon as the deepest snowdrifts
had melted and the wind had warmed, Scotty was off. He said
goodbye to his friends, took the small savings he had accumulated
in the Custer bank, and rode south.

Camp Robinson was much more lively and interesting than
Fort Fetterman. By the time Scotty arrived in April there were
many Indians camped near the Red Cloud agency. With his previous experience, Scotty had no trouble signing on as a government teamster and scout at the nearby military post.

Then, only a few days after he started working, news came
that Crook was on his way to the fort—with Crazy Horse!

5

Crazy On a cool May morning, Scotty stood with most of
Horse the population of Camp Robinson watching the
white bluffs to the north.

They waited quietly. The white soldiers and scouts around
Scotty chatted together; the Indian women and children nearby
were silent. On top of the bluffs Red Cloud's men were silhou-
etted against the sky, their horses standing motionless.

Scotty leaned against a scrubby cottonwood tree and talked
with Cornie Utterback, another teamster with whom he had become friendly. Cornie was a Virginian, a muscular little man who
doubled as a blacksmith. He punctuated his soft southern speech
by spitting out the pumpkin seeds he liked to chew.

"Angus can live anywhere," Scotty said, carrying on a long-
standing argument on the merits of different breeds of cattle.
"They don't have to be babied, they can stand snow and cold."

"They can't travel like longhorns," Cornie insisted. "You have
to get 'em to market, and that's where . . . Look! Here they
come!"

The mounted Indians on the bluffs were moving, blending in
with a line of horsemen coming over the top of the trail and down
into the valley. A great cloud of dust rose around them as they
wound closer. Scotty and Cornie edged through the crowd beside
the trail to get a better look.

At the head of the procession rode Lieutenant Clark, called "White Hat" by the Indians, and the dignified Red Cloud. Scotty strained to see the man who rode alone behind them, for of course this must be the famous Crazy Horse.

He was surprisingly young and small. Scotty noticed a scar on his face. There was something reserved, almost mysterious about his expression; Scotty remembered that the Oglala Sioux called him their "Strange Man." He was dressed very plainly, with no paint and only a single feather in his hair. His long braids were wrapped in fur of some kind.

Behind Crazy Horse rode his headmen, behind them the rest of the warriors, and finally the women and children who had been traveling with them. The procession reached far back down the valley and over the distant bluffs. As the Indians approached the fort they began to sing, their heads thrown back and their voices rich and deep.

The music was of unfamiliar beat and tone, the words incomprehensible, but the impression was one of power and faith. This did not look like a beaten people marching in to surrender, but like men who had indeed defeated Crook and Custer and the best soldiers the whites had.

"Those are Cheyennes," Charlie said, pointing to a group of warriors riding together not far behind Crazy Horse. "I've seen some of their chiefs here before: Hog, Little Wolf, and there's Dull Knife leading them."

"Why are they with the Sioux?" Scotty asked.

"Sioux and Cheyennes have always been friendly. They fight together, take care of each other."

The Cheyenne men, like the Sioux, carried their shields proudly. They were handsome people. Scotty liked the way they sat their horses, the strength and defiance in their faces. He wondered whether any of them had been among the warriors who had driven the cavalry out of Two Moons' camp.

It was late afternoon before the "hostiles" had all come in and camped around the agency. As he looked after the livestock that evening, Scotty listened to the peculiar beat of their singing and wondered what the songs were about.

His preparations for the move to Camp Robinson had been simple, and he had brought only the few essentials that would go in his bedroll. After feeding the horses that evening he strolled to the trader's cabin to look for a new razor, a hat, some towels, and other things he would need.

Long Joe Larribee was one of the first men Scotty had met at Camp Robinson. Half French, half Indian, he supplied both the soldiers and the Sioux with goods they wanted. His cabin stood between the fort and the agency, and tonight it was crowded with shoppers.

Scotty stood for awhile outside the cabin, listening to the talk about the events of the day. There were many Indians and half-breeds there, as well as white soldiers and scouts, and the murmur of their speech blended with the English Scotty understood.

Suddenly a heavyset, red-haired man stamped through the front door of the trader's cabin and into the yard. He was dragging a small boy by the arm. The boy could not have been more than four or five years old.

"No son of mine will be a thief," the man roared. "I saw you take that mirror." He picked up a large stick from the ground and began to beat the boy with it.

The child did not cry at first. His face was pale, his eyes screwed up, and Scotty could almost feel him struggling to keep still. For that moment Scotty was back in Morayshire, in the yard behind the stone farmhouse, and his own father was applying the beating. "Spare the rod and spoil the child"—he had heard that often enough.

When the little boy finally cried, Scotty looked away, hurting with him. And his eyes met those of a beautiful young Indian girl standing only a few yards from him. She was watching with a look of anger and disgust.

Scotty looked around at the other Indians nearby, and they all seemed shocked, disbelieving. When the white man put down the stick and walked away with his son, the Indians stared after them and spoke softly to each other.

Scotty turned back to the Indian girl he had first observed. She was holding a tiny baby in her arms and rocking it, stroking its head. Impulsively he asked her, "Do you speak any English?"

"Yes." She looked at him with distaste.

"What are the people saying about that man?"

"They say the white man must be crazy. Only a crazy person would beat a child."

"But if your children need to be punished . . ."

She held the baby tighter. "We do not punish our children. The little boy saw a pretty thing and picked it up. What father would strike him for that?" She turned and walked gracefully into the trader's cabin.

"See you met one of the Larribee girls." Cornie Utterback strolled up beside Scotty.

"Is she the trader's daughter?"

"One of 'em. There's four, each one prettier than the last. Their mother was a Cheyenne woman. The one with the baby is called Sally."

"She seems young to be married." Scotty was not sure why he was asking so many questions, but the girl interested him.

"*Was* married. To some half-breed who turned out to be a skunk, went off and left her alone with that baby."

"The Indians all seemed so amazed at that whipping—is it true that they never punish their children?"

"I've been here a year, and I never saw an Indian parent lift a finger against a child."

"But how do they control them?"

Cornie shrugged and popped a pumpkin seed into his mouth. "Just plain love, I guess. Never saw people who love kids like they do. There's always some aunt or uncle or grandparent to pick up a fussy baby, and the older boys and girls seem to want to copy their parents and the other grown people. I don't know, maybe they've got the right idea. You never see Indian kids running away from home, like I did, or growing up hating their folks."

Later, when they were doing their trading in the cabin, Scotty caught several glimpses of Sally Larribee and another girl who looked like a sister. Once he noticed Cornie talking with the two of them.

In the weeks that followed, Scotty watched the Indian people around the fort and the agency. He had never really thought of them as people before, with habits and traditions, religion and law and family customs. He saw all these things now—heard them laughing together, heard their wails of grief at the death of loved ones.

With Cornie's help he learned to speak a few words of Dakota. "Sioux" was not really the proper name for these Indians, Cornie told him, it was a name given them by their enemies. They called themselves Dakotas or Lakotas.

Shortly after Crazy Horse and his followers came to the agency, the Cheyennes who had been with them were sent away again. The United States government had decreed that they should join the southern branch of the Cheyenne tribe in Indian territory. Scotty heard that Dull Knife and the other Cheyenne chiefs had pleaded to be allowed to stay in the north, where they had always lived. Crazy Horse and the Dakotas also asked the soldiers to let their Cheyenne brothers stay, but the decision had already been made.

So on another summer morning, Scotty watched the Cheyennes ride out again—not so proudly this time. Their weapons were gone, and they were escorted by a heavy army guard. Turning back toward the stables after they had disappeared down the trail, Scotty caught a glimpse of a man standing alone, motionless. It was Crazy Horse.

The Dakota chief stared after the Cheyennes. Scotty wondered whether he was asking himself, Is this what they have planned for me, too? For there were rumors around the fort that Crazy Horse was too dangerous to be left with his people, that he would be imprisoned somewhere.

Scotty wanted to get away from Camp Robinson, at least for the summer. There was no future in his work there, and he was depressed by the atmosphere. The soldiers were bored; the Indians were idle and frustrated.

Cornie Utterback told Scotty about a cattle outfit on the Running Water, just a short distance from Camp Robinson. On the first of July, Scotty drew his pay and rode out to look for work as a cowboy.

The summer was lonely, but when it was over Scotty felt sure that he had become a man. He spent his days with no one to talk to, his nights on ground so cold his teeth chattered.

One night, all alone on the vast prairie, he noticed a weird light playing around the horns of the cattle. He thought he was dreaming or delirious until he remembered seeing the same eerie light around the masts of ships in the harbor back in Scotland. St. Elmo's fire! He had never understood what made the glow, but he knew it heralded a storm.

The cattle ran with the first loud crack of thunder, and Scotty spent the whole night just trying to stay with them. Prairie fires sputtered and blazed, set off by the lightning, and then were drenched by the rain that followed. When the sun rose, Scotty could find only about a dozen of the fifty or more longhorns he had been guarding.

It took a week to round up the missing cattle. By that time it was September, and Scotty was ready for a rest from the grueling work. Dirty, tired, and shabby, he rode back into Camp Robinson.

He had completely worn out a saddle that summer. Shortly after coming back to his old bunk at the fort, he washed, shaved, and walked to trader Larribee's to look for a new one.

Midafternoon was a slack time at the trader's. There was just one old Indian there when Scotty arrived, a man named Broken Arm. Scotty had often seen him standing around the trader's and had practiced his few words of Dakota on him.

"How kola," Scotty said, trying to get the proper tone in his greeting.

"How kola," answered Broken Arm gravely.

Searching for something else to say, Scotty noticed a beaded medallion the old man was wearing around his neck. It was of the thunderbird design the Dakotas used so much, done in blue, yellow, red and white. Scotty pointed to it and tried to remember the word for "good" or "beautiful," to make some kind of compliment. Finally he just smiled and looked admiring.

Broken Arm beamed. Before Scotty realized what he was doing, the old man took the medallion off and handed it to him.

"Ah . . . how much?" Again, the Dakota words would not come to Scotty. He had not intended to buy the ornament, but he did not want to insult Broken Arm.

The Indian kept on smiling and nodding until Scotty dug into his pocket and drew out a silver dollar. But Broken Arm made no move to take the money.

"He doesn't want to be paid."

Scotty turned and saw Sally Larribee standing behind him.

"But this is a beautiful thing. Why should he give it to me? I hardly know him."

"You admired it. He's being generous, so just take it. You'll hurt his feelings if you don't."

Scotty pantomimed his gratitude and Broken Arm shuffled out, looking pleased.

"Buying and selling doesn't mean anything to Indians," Sally told him. She moved gracefully behind the counter and leaned over it, her chin in her hands. "You know when we try to say 'I sold it' in Dakota, it comes out 'I *gave* it.' 'I bought this' is translated 'I took this.' "

"Doesn't that give your father some problems?"

"Sometimes. But most of the Dakotas understand trading, so we just do that instead of trying to use money."

"Speaking of money, I want to buy a saddle. Do you have any?"

Sally led him to a corner of the cabin where several leather saddles were piled. As he examined them, Scotty also watched the trader's daughter. She had the broad forehead and full mouth of the Cheyennes. Her eyes were set deep and shadowed by heavy lashes, and her long straight hair was a lustrous black. He could see no evidence of the French blood he knew she must have on her father's side, unless her skin was a trifle lighter in color than that of the fullbloods.

He selected a reddish saddle that was only slightly worn. As he paid for it, he tried to strike up the conversation again: "I've been learning a little Dakota, but so far I don't speak it very well. Do you think you could help me some time? If I could practice with someone who knows both English and Dakota . . ."

"Why would you want to learn?" Her face was closed again, indifferent. She turned away to wait on a group of young officers who had come into the store.

That night as they finished grooming and feeding the horses, Scotty and Cornie Utterback had a chance to exchange the summer's news. Cornie described the current feuds among some of the officers at the fort, the excitement caused by a visit from Buffalo Bill Cody, who was recruiting Indians for his Wild West show, and the persistent rumors that Crazy Horse was to be removed from the agency soon.

"Didn't Crook promise him his own reservation, up in the Powder River country?" Scotty asked.

"Yep, and I suppose he meant it, too, but he couldn't get the government to go along. I heard he went all the way to Washington about it—but those politicians don't care about a few Indians."

"Do you think Crazy Horse might start trouble?"

"Don't see any sign of it so far. He took another wife this summer, you know—one of those Larribee girls."

For some reason Scotty was startled. "Which . . ."

"Nellie, the oldest. He already had one wife, Black Robe Woman. She's got TB and is pretty sick, they say."

"Well, did he leave her, then?"

"Oh, no, the Dakotas sometimes do take two wives. The younger one can do some of the work for Black Robe Woman. They don't seem to get jealous like white women would."

From the moment he rode into Camp Robinson, Crazy Horse had been a hero, almost a god, to the Indian people there. Scotty had seen the way they looked at him and murmured his name—always with awe. There was no one else who commanded that kind of respect. Even popular leaders like Red Cloud held power only when people were willing to follow them, and Scotty had noticed that the Indians were quite independent in their thinking. But Crazy Horse seemed to be set apart from the bickering and disagreement among the others. He was special.

A few days later a council was held at the agency. Crook wanted to recruit some of the Dakotas to go north and fight against the Nez Perce Indians. After that council, rumors were more confusing than ever. Some claimed that Crazy Horse had refused and had threatened instead to go to war against the whites. Others insisted that an interpreter named Grouard had deliberately misquoted Crazy Horse to Crook, that Crazy Horse had actually agreed but Crook thought he had said something quite different. In any case, most of the men Scotty talked with were sure that Crook was very angry with Crazy Horse and that something would happen soon.

Early one morning Scotty walked down to the creek to get water for shaving. He had wakened sooner than usual; the clouds in the east were just beginning to show pink. He stumbled over a rock half-hidden in shadow and splashed water across the path. He paused a moment to dry himself off, and when he started forward again he almost collided with Sally Larribee.

He had not seen her approaching. Even in the poor light, he could see that she was upset. There were tears in her eyes, and her long hair hung loose down her back.

"What's wrong?" he blurted, realizing the moment the words were out of his mouth that he did not know her well enough to ask. Still, he wanted to know.

"You haven't heard the soldiers? They're coming for Crazy Horse." She smiled scornfully. "They won't find him, though—not this time."

Now Scotty realized why he had wakened so early. There had been a stirring in one of the barracks, the sound of men and horses. He had assumed it was just a small patrol starting off on a journey.

"You mean he's to be arrested?" Scotty asked.

Sally nodded. "We found out last night. My sister warned her husband, and he escaped. When the soldiers reach the camp, they'll find it empty. I'm waiting to see them when they return without him!" Again she smiled, but there was no joy in her face.

He heard horses coming down the trail from the agency, and then as the sun appeared above the horizon he could see the soldiers. He counted eight troops of cavalry; they even had a cannon with them.

"You *wasichus* send many soldiers to a people you've already disarmed," Sally commented.

Scotty wanted to answer. He did not like being lumped together with the *wasichus,* the whites, as if he agreed with everything they did. But he could not think of a good reply, and when he turned back from watching the last of the cavalry pass by he saw that Sally had gone away as silently as she had come.

It was a long day, a long night. The fort was put under heavy guard, and a large troop rode out in pursuit of Crazy Horse. Cornie said that Crazy Horse would be sent to prison at the Dry Tortugas when he was captured, that there was a special train waiting for that purpose.

The next day a message came through that Lieutenant Jesse Lee was bringing Crazy Horse back from the Spotted Tail agency. There had been no battle; somehow the "Strange Man" had been persuaded to come back peacefully. Scotty wondered whether he had been told what the soldiers had in mind for him.

Through the afternoon the open area at the fort filled up with Indians, milling around, talking, waiting. Scotty tried to keep busy. He mended harness, helped the blacksmith awhile and checked the injured leg of one of the horses.

Cornie found him in the stable. "Crazy Horse just rode in," Cornie said.

Something told Scotty not to go. But though he had no desire to see the Dakota chief humiliated, he could not resist the itch of simple curiosity. He followed Cornie out into the yard.

The crowd was immense, but Scotty could see over their heads

to the little group of men in front of the guardhouse. Crazy
Horse was with Little Big Man, a scout, and a guard of some
twenty soldiers. As Scotty watched, a young lieutenant motioned
to Crazy Horse and the Indian followed him into the guardhouse.
It seemed incredible that he would make no resistance and would
go so meekly into captivity.

Then the guardhouse door burst open again. Crazy Horse
plunged through it, waving two knives and shouting. The crowd
stirred and shoved forward. Some of the scouts leveled their guns
at Crazy Horse. Little Big Man grabbed one of his arms, a soldier
the other.

Then Scotty saw another of the guards lift his gun and plunge
the fixed bayonet into Crazy Horse's back.

6

Chi-Chi's A flock of wild geese filled the cold air with
Daughter their gabbling. Scotty watched them soaring
across the clouds, heading south in some intricate formation that
only they understood. The wind stiffened, and Scotty shivered
and pulled his wool jacket tighter around his shoulders.

"Hey! Ha!" he yelled, moving the small herd of cattle back
toward the protection of a draw. There was snow in the air, snow
in the grey clouds above, and no telling how much would fall before the storm was over.

After the killing of Crazy Horse, the atmosphere at Camp
Robinson had become unbearable. The Indians, sullen and angry,
kept to themselves. Somehow a major uprising was avoided, but
any trust there had been between the Dakotas and their captors
was destroyed. The soldiers were also suspicious and resentful.
They fought among themselves, drank too much, and applied for
transfers to more interesting posts.

Then a new order was issued from Washington: the Dakotas
were to move to their permanent reservations. An agency for
Red Cloud's Oglala band was to be built, another for Spotted
Tail's Brules. Rations and supplies promised in the treaties would
be distributed from these agencies.

So most of the Indians who had been camped around the fort

Chief Red Cloud's Oglala people followed him to a new agency on the forks of the White River in 1877.

were gone by late fall. Red Cloud's people had moved to the forks of the White River, Spotted Tail's group farther south on the same river.

Scotty put his savings together with some money furnished by a young fellow named George Clark, and bought a few head of longhorn cattle. They were stringy and thin, but Scotty hoped that he could make enough on them to start his own ranch someday.

George Clark turned out to be a rather invisible partner. He left soon after they bought the cattle to make a trip north with a load of freight to sell in the gold mining camps; when he did come back it was only to "see how we're doing."

Scotty built a crude dugout eight miles north of Camp Robinson on the Black Hills road, over the Nebraska line in Dakota Territory. He roofed it with branches and sod, brought in a few pieces of used furniture and built a fireplace of stones with a hole in the roof to let the smoke out.

Now winter was coming on, and he was alone. He maneuvered the cattle into the draw and left them there, hoping they could survive the storm. He tied his pony in the lean-to beside the dugout and went inside, chilled and bone-tired.

That night he lay awake for hours. The wind howled over the dugout like the ghosts in a hundred childhood tales. Trying to sleep, Scotty imagined himself seeking his fortune in South America. As soon as spring came he would buy a steamship ticket for Buenos Aires. He would not spend another winter in this wilderness.

The storm had blown itself out by morning, and Scotty found the cattle huddled together in the draw where he had left them. They were tough, he had to admit that. As one blizzard followed another, most of them lived on, munching prairie grass where they found it in sheltered spots.

For Scotty the only breaks in the monotony were his occasional trips to Camp Robinson for supplies. The following afternoon he had had enough of solitude, so he took advantage of the milder weather to ride into the settlement. Shortly after noon he stood on the porch in front of Long Joe Larribee's store, shaking the snow off his coat and brushing tiny icicles from his frozen eyebrows and moustache.

"You look like you've been rolling in the snowdrifts, the way my Posey likes to do." Sally Larribee held the door open for him. Her little boy, Posey, now a fat two-year-old, was just emerging from a fluffy pile of snow, squealing with delight.

Scotty laughed and stamped his boots clean. "Sometimes I think I *live* in a snowdrift. That dugout of mine isn't much better than a hollowed-out drift." He followed her into the store.

"What do you need, Mr. Philip?" She moved quietly among the stacks of merchandise.

"Sunshine, I guess. Could you sell me about a quart of that?"

"I'm sorry, we don't have any in stock. Maybe by the end of the winter you'll understand why the sun is so important to us in this part of the country."

"Cornie Utterback told me about the big Sun Dance they have each summer. I'd like to see it."

Sally looked away, suddenly not so friendly. "What did you want to buy today?"

Scotty paid for his flour, bacon, coffee, kerosene and corn meal. As he was bundling them up and getting ready to leave, two of Sally's sisters came in with the snow-drenched Posey. The three of them changed Posey's wet clothes and chattered in Dakota, ignoring the white intruder. Scotty still did not know enough of the language to catch the meaning of their soft words. Then the other two went through the back door into the part of the house where the Larribee family lived, and Sally picked up Posey and began to rock him and sing to him:

A wa wa
I ni na
I sti ma na.

Scotty had his coat on and his purchases under his arm. But he did not want to leave. He thought of the long days ahead, the loneliness, the silence—he had to try once more for some kind of conversation with the Indian woman.

"What does that mean, the song you're singing?" he asked her.

She looked up at him, the child in her arms already asleep. "It's just a song, what you would call a lullaby."

"Tell me the words."

" 'I ni na' means 'be still'; 'i sti ma na,' 'sleep.' That's all there is to it: be still, sleep."

"I like the song."

"My mother used to sing it to me, when I was very small. I remember her singing it at night, in the dark. The Dakotas called her Shahunwinla, that means Cheyenne Woman, but her name among the Cheyennes was 'Chi-Chi.' " Sally broke off, looking embarrassed. It was the most Scotty had ever heard her say at one time.

The front door was hurled open then, and with a blast of cold air, a group of cavalrymen stamped in. Sally laid her sleeping child on a pile of fur robes at the side of the store and went to wait on them.

Scotty rode back to the dugout slowly, dreading the sight and smoky smell of it. As he rode the Indian lullaby hummed through his head.

George Clark arrived from his freighting trip the day before

Christmas, so at least Scotty did not have to spend the holiday
alone. As soon as the weather cleared again, Scotty left with a
load of freight for Custer, and Clark stayed behind to tend the
stock.

Freighting was hard work, especially in winter. The mules had
to scramble up the icy trails or struggle through mudholes and
snowbanks, with Scotty helping them along as best he could. Several times on that trip the wagon tipped and fell on its side, and he
had to reload all the goods and repair the damage to the wagon.
He was lucky in the weather. There was only one storm, and that
a very slight one.

The things he took to sell in the hills were all much in demand
there, and he got good prices for everything. Prospectors waiting
out the boredom of winter were as eager for news as they were
for supplies. Scotty told them everything he had heard or read at
Camp Robinson. He had no desire to go back to mining after
spending a few hours with the discouraged, homesick, quarrel-
some men in the Black Hills.

But it was fun to see how Custer had changed. The first boom
was over; many prospectors had moved on to the richer mines
around Deadwood Gulch, and those who stayed in the southern
hills were beginning to look like permanent residents. Scotty
even saw a few elegantly gowned women there, wives of busi-
nessmen who had made a success of their first years in the West.

Looking at the women's tightly-bound "wasp waists," their
fancy dresses and hats, their cool white faces, Scotty thought of
Sally Larribee. There was something so different about her—not
just the color of her skin and hair or the clothes she wore.

Pasqueflowers were blooming when Scotty got back to the
dugout. He and George worked together branding the newborn

calves and checking their winter losses. They agreed that George, who liked the variety and travel of freighting, would handle that end of the partnership during the summer. Scotty would stay near Camp Robinson and take care of the cattle. He also had an idea to add to their savings: he would cut and bale the abundant range grass and sell it to the Army as feed for animals during the coming winter.

One morning a few days after George left, Scotty was working on a larger shelter he was building for horses near the dugout and the original lean-to. Turning at the sound of hoofbeats, he saw Cornie Utterback riding up.

"Cornie!" Scotty yelled, dropping his hammer. "Haven't seen you for months. Come in and have a cup of coffee."

"If that dugout's as smoky and stuffy as usual, I'd as soon bring the coffee out here," Cornie said. "Sun's warm enough."

So they sat under the lone tree on Scotty's place, drank their steaming coffee and exchanged news.

"I've been freighting for the Army all winter," Cornie said. "Hauling rations for the Indians that are still around here and supplies for the soldiers. Made four trips to the Missouri and back."

"You'd have made more money doing it on your own, like we did," Scotty teased.

"Maybe so, but the work's steady and they furnish all the equipment."

"You do any freighting to Red Cloud's camp, or Spotted Tail's?"

"Stopped once at each place. They're doing most of the hauling from the river themselves—when there's something to haul." Cornie spat. "As usual, our Uncle Sam's finding it a bit hard to keep his promises to the Dakotas."

"There's no trouble brewing with the Indians, is there?"

"Trouble? Those people haven't even got enough to eat, and half of 'em have been sick this winter with smallpox and measles. Most every family's lost a child or an old grandma. They're in no shape to make trouble."

Scotty sipped his coffee in silence, listening to the gentle noises of the cattle grazing nearby. Finally he asked his friend, "You still living at the fort? I might drop in and see you in a few days . . ."

Cornie stood up. "No, I'm not there any more. I've got a little cabin near the agency. Ask at Larribee's store, they can tell you which one it is." He started to unhitch his horse from the tree branch. "Fact is, I got married."

"Married?" Scotty felt his mouth drop open. "But who—"

"Zoe Larribee." Cornie swung up on his horse and laced the reins through the fingers of one hand.

"Oh. Well, that's fine. Congratulations. I . . . never thought you'd . . . I mean I thought you were the bachelor type."

Scotty hated himself for stumbling and stammering, but he was too surprised to know what to say. He knew, of course, that some of the soldiers had become interested in Indian girls, and a few had even married them. But then the soldiers would be transferred and often the Indian-style weddings forgotten and the Indian wives left behind. He wondered whether Cornie would be as casual about his new Indian wife.

It took Scotty more than a few days to get around to visiting the Utterbacks' new home. In fact, it was a month later when Scotty finally strolled across the path from the old agency to their cabin. The summer sun beat down on his back, and his boots crunched over the dry ground.

Zoe answered his knock. She looked at him a little suspiciously at first, but invited him inside. The cabin was small and not too well constructed. Scotty had to stand with his head bent awkwardly to avoid bumping it against the ceiling. The windows were covered with transparent paper. Everything was very clean and neat.

"I'm sorry," Zoe said, "we were just getting ready to leave. Cornie's out back packing the wagon now. I'll call him . . ."

"Don't bother, if you're going someplace. I'll come another time."

But Cornie had noticed Scotty's horse and was already coming through the door. "Hey, Scotchman, we're going up north to see the big Sun Dance. Why don't you come along?"

"Well, I don't know—how long will you be gone?"

"Just today. The dance goes on for a week or more, but I've got to get back to start on a freighting trip Wednesday. How about it?"

Scotty laughed. "Why not? I was going to stay around Camp Robinson for a couple of days anyway. George got back and he's there to watch the cattle. All right, I'll come."

It was not until Cornie brought the wagon around to the front of the cabin that Scotty saw there was someone in it. Sally Larribee was sitting on a buffalo robe in the wagon bed, her black hair shining in the sunlight.

"Zoe's sister's going with us, too," Cornie said. "You know her, don't you?"

Scotty nodded, and Sally smiled faintly at him. Zoe got into the back with her sister, and the two men climbed to the high seat.

They took turns driving Cornie's team of black mares. Even the main road was bumpy. After they left it to follow a little-used trail to the Indian camp, the wagon bounced along at a bone-jarring pace. Clouds of dust clogged Scotty's throat and made his eyes water. He was glad when they heard the Indian drums in the distance.

Cornie hobbled the horses near the edge of the great circle of tepees. Scotty walked beside Sally, following Cornie and Zoe, toward the sound of the drums.

"Have you been to one of these before?" Scotty asked.

"Yes, many times. There is one every summer." Sally looked straight ahead.

"Will you explain to me what's going on in the Sun Dance? I don't know much about it."

"It's a religious ceremony. I don't think I *could* explain it to . . ."

Scotty was peeved by her attitude. He stepped in front of her, forcing her to stop and face him. "You act as if I were pure poison," he said. "I can't help being white! Your father's part white, isn't he?"

Sally looked at him for a moment, then looked away again. When she spoke, her voice was warmer. "It's just that I've seen other *wasichus* come to Indian ceremonies to make fun of the 'poor savages.' Or else they're shocked by the Sun Dance because they don't understand. I'm sorry. I shouldn't blame you for what others have done." Then she smiled, and chuckled to herself.

"What's so funny?"

"Just what you said about how you couldn't help being white. And my father. Do you know he thinks you're a half-breed too?"

"Me?" Scotty was dumbfounded. "I grew up in Scotland!"

"But you do have dark skin, and that black hair . . ."

Scotty had to laugh too. "I guess you're right. I never thought of it. That's the Spanish blood in me—the Philip family was founded by a Spaniard who was shipwrecked in Scotland. So I suppose I am a half-breed, in a way."

Cornie motioned to them to join the crowd of onlookers around the clearing where the dance was going on. Scotty and Sally moved as close as they could, and immediately the spectacle had their full attention.

In the center of the clearing was a pole with a crossbar. A buffalo skull and a decorated pipe lay on the ground beneath it. The dancers circled around the pole, their bodies painted red, blue, yellow, white and black. Their hair was not braided, but hung loosely over their shoulders. They were barefoot, and wore only breechcloths of white deerskin.

Some of the dancers had buffalo skulls hanging by thongs, which were fastened to sticks thrust through the flesh of their arms or backs. A few were linked by thongs to the central pole, with the sticks piercing their chests, and had to dance almost on their toes, their backs arched.

"Are they prisoners, or criminals, or what?" Scotty whispered to Sally.

"No, nothing like that," she replied. "They made vows. The piercing isn't forced on anyone."

All the men who were dancing had whistles which they blew, and as they circled they kept their faces always toward the sun. The onlookers sang, and their song somehow reminded Scotty of the wail of bagpipes. He noticed how reverent all the Indian people were. They seemed totally absorbed in worship—much more so than the drowsy congregations Scotty remembered in Sunday morning church.

A buffalo skull fell from the back of one of the dancers. A woman rushed out and poured some sort of powder into the wound, and soon the man was dancing again. Later, some of those suspended from the pole fell to the ground, their flesh torn by the motion of the dance. They were treated with the same powder.

It was dusk when Cornie decided they would have to leave. When they got to the wagon, Scotty said casually, "I'll ride in back with Sally awhile. I want to ask her about the dance. You let me know when you want me to drive."

Cornie smiled. "I think I can make it back all right."

The evening was clear and cool. Stars upon stars stretched out over the openness of the plains, and the summer moon softened the dark. For a while no one spoke. That was one of the things Scotty liked about Sally—with her, silence was comfortable.

"Tell me about the dance," Scotty asked finally. "Do the Dakotas think of the sun as a god?"

"Not exactly as a god, not the way you think of God. But to us
everything is *wakan,* holy. And the sun is the most holy of all, because it gives light and warmth and everything people need to
live. We do worship the sun, and the earth, our mother, and the
buffalo, and many other things. More important than even the
sun is *wakan tanka,* the Mysterious One, the creator."

"But why do the dancers cut and torture themselves like that?
Do they think it will please the sun, or this 'Mysterious One'?"

Sally sighed and ran a hand over her hair. "It's hard to explain.
Indians believe that the things on earth are gifts which we just
use; we don't own them. The only thing a man can possess is his
own body. So when he wants to express something very deep he
gives the only thing that belongs to him; his flesh, his pain. That's
why Indians sometimes cut themselves to show their grief after
the death of a relative."

"I never thought of it that way," Scotty said. "I guess it makes
sense. But why all the buffalo skulls used in the dance? Aren't the
buffalo pretty much gone around here? I haven't seen a dozen
since I've lived in Nebraska."

"Yes, they are gone. But not from the Dakota religion. You
don't realize what buffalo meant to our people: food, clothes, shelter, tools, trade goods—almost everything we needed." She was
quiet for a moment, then spoke again very softly. "You know,
some of our people believe that when the last buffalo dies the
Dakotas will disappear from the earth."

Scotty had no reply for that. He remembered the acres of rotting buffalo he had seen in Kansas, the piles of bones all over the
Great Plains. He leaned back in the swaying wagon, watching
the sky wheel by and conscious of the woman beside him.

He was beginning to see things through her eyes. He found

himself questioning ideas he had accepted all his life, and other beliefs that seemed to be part of his new country. Was religion necessarily a matter of dressing up on Sunday morning and spending hours in a hard pew? Were Indians really the savages he had been told they were? Or did they possibly understand something about life that he had never even thought about?

He told himself it really didn't matter. Next spring, if all went as he hoped, he would be leaving. The freighting business was prospering. He was able to earn extra money with other jobs. Soon he would have enough to buy land somewhere, and all this would probably be forgotten. After all, he had never intended to stay here.

As they neared Camp Robinson, Scotty thought of Sally's child. "Who's taking care of Posey?" he asked.

"My sister." Sally seemed surprised at the question.

"Where is . . . Posey's father now?"

"Louis Moran left before he was born. I haven't seen him since." There was bitterness in her tone.

"But doesn't he help you support the child?"

"When a marriage ends, the child belongs to the mother. That's the Dakota tradition. Of course, Louis is half white and he doesn't care anything for traditions," she said fiercely, the hurt sounding under her words. "I was very young when I married him," she added.

The wagon rattled over the last hill and stopped in front of Long Joe Larribee's cabin. Scotty got out and helped Sally down. He told her good night rather awkwardly and rode on to the Utterbacks' cabin to spend the night there.

He didn't see Sally again that summer. Most of the time he was busy with the cattle and the hay; on the few trips he made to Larribee's, Long Joe or his wife waited on Scotty.

One evening late in September George Clark came galloping

into Camp Robinson and found Scotty just coming out of the store.

"You look like you've got some news," Scotty said. "What happened?"

"I just heard about it down at Rushville," George said, sliding off his sweaty horse. "Remember that bunch of Cheyennes that came in with Crazy Horse? The ones they sent to Indian Territory? They've escaped, and they're heading up here! The Army will be sending troops, and they'll need scouts. What do you say we sign up?"

"It's been too quiet around here lately," Scotty said. "Let's go."

7

Songs of Scotty yanked on the reins and stopped his pony
Death at the top of a rise, trying to get his bearings.
Stinging bits of snow struck his face. He squinted in the direction
he thought was east, looking for some familiar landmark—but
there was nothing. Only snow swirling, drifting, burying the
earth.

The pony struggled forward again at Scotty's urging. The soldiers had to be within a few miles of this spot; Scotty had seen
signs of their camp just before the blizzard struck. He was carrying a dispatch to Major Carlton, whose men were still looking for
the missing Cheyennes.

This was Scotty's third trip carrying dispatches to and from
Camp Robinson since the hunt for the Cheyennes had begun.
Still Dull Knife, Little Wolf and the others evaded the soldiers.

The first reports out of Kansas had indicated a full-scale Indian
war, with hundreds of whites massacred, farms burned, horses
and cattle stolen. Later Scotty heard that the stories had been ex-
aggerated. The Indians had stolen food, and a few white ranchers
had been killed trying to stop them—that was all.

Camp Robinson was on alert because of the rumor that the
Cheyennes were heading that way. Actually, they were going
home. Scotty remembered how the Indians had tried to persuade
the army not to send them south in the first place.

They would be worthy enemies, if Major Carlton's men ever found them. Scotty remembered how the Cheyenne warriors had looked that day he had watched them ride into Camp Robinson with Crazy Horse. The Cheyennes were sometimes called the "Beautiful People" by other tribes, and it was easy to see why. Scotty pictured again their fine features, the easy grace with which they rode, and their lean, muscular bodies. It was no wonder they had outfought the U.S. Army four times just since they had left Indian Territory!

The wind howled. At first Scotty thought he was imagining the sound of human voices, then he saw dim shapes ahead, men and horses. He had found the cavalry.

"Where's the major?" he asked the first soldier he saw.

"Up ahead, checking the prisoners."

"Prisoners? You mean you found the Cheyennes?"

The young soldier nodded. "Just this morning. We sort of stumbled across them in the snow. Guess now we can get back to camp and warm up; those barracks will sure look good."

"Was there any fighting?"

"Nope—they put up the white flag right away."

Scotty felt surprised and vaguely let down. It was not, he told himself, that he wanted to see a lot of killing. But he had expected some sort of action after all the publicity on the Cheyenne escape, perhaps something exciting to write back to his family in Kansas. . . . He rode on through groups of shivering soldiers, some standing close to the campfires, others huddled on their horses.

Then he saw the Cheyennes. They stood together, surrounded by guards. There were more women and children than men, and none of them looked anything like the fierce warriors Scotty had been remembering. They were dressed in rags. Their faces were gaunt, their limbs bony. Some of the children were whimpering softly; all the Cheyennes looked like they were near starvation.

Scotty drew the dispatch case from inside his heavy coat and got down from his horse. He walked through the snow to the major, who was standing nearby with some of his officers.

"Message from Camp Robinson," Scotty said, handing the dispatch to Major Carlton.

"Good," said the major. "You can go back and tell them we caught the Indians. Two of our companies came across them this morning, and they surrendered without a fight. Wait, I'll write down a report for you to take to Camp Robinson."

The major walked toward a large tent that had been put up nearby, glancing at Scotty's dispatches as he went.

Scotty warmed himself by a fire. He glanced at the Cheyennes, and then tried not to look at them. He thought of the journey they had made—nearly six hundred miles. He wondered how they had ever managed to escape all the white soldiers who had been looking for them, how they had crossed western Kansas and the rugged Nebraska sandhills.

Someone offered Scotty a mug of coffee, and he took it gratefully. As he swallowed the last of the hot liquid he saw one of the Indian women watching him, her face pinched and drawn. He looked away.

"Has anybody given them food or drink?" Scotty asked a young soldier who was standing near him.

"Not yet," the soldier said. "Just found 'em this morning. I think the major plans to pass out some kind of rations before we start the march to Robinson. They've come this far, they ought to be able to make it a few more miles."

One of the major's aides found Scotty then and gave him back the dispatch case, with a new message to be delivered to Captain Henry Wessells, commanding officer at the post. Scotty traded his pony for a fresh mount and set out.

The Cheyennes and their soldier guard arrived at Camp Robinson two days after Scotty brought news of their capture. He saw them come in, limping, huddled in their ragged clothing, yet somehow still undefeated. They were given quarters in an empty barracks on the army post, and for the time being no decision was announced as to what would be done with them. Newspapers were still blaring the stories of their "crimes," and Scotty knew that the state of Kansas was demanding that they be returned for trial there. Army officials were infuriated by their disobedience and wanted to make an example of them. Still, no one would say what was to be done.

The early snow melted away for the time being, and Scotty became busy baling more hay and delivering it to the post. He picked out some of their cattle to sell, and George drove them up to the Black Hills where he had found a buyer. While his partner was gone Scotty worked hard repairing the dugout and the outbuildings on the ranch.

On Christmas Day, 1878, Scotty had dinner with the Utterbacks. Cornie had been out to the ranch a week before to invite him, and he was glad he didn't have to spend the holiday alone. Also at the dinner were Long Joe Larribee, his second wife, their five small sons, Sally, and her little boy, Posey.

The meal was noisy but cheerful. It had been a long time since Scotty had eaten with a real family. He enjoyed the giggles and confusion. Zoe had fixed a huge platter of Indian fry bread to go with the roast beef and vegetables; Scotty ate until he could not hold another bite. He watched Sally helping the little ones with their food, settling quarrels between her half-brothers, and clearing the table for Zoe when everyone was through.

The children were bundled up and sent outside to play. Scotty eased himself into a hand-made wooden chair and rubbed his stomach. "That's the best meal I've had since I left Kansas," he said.

"Zoe's a good cook," Cornie said contentedly. "Well, Long Joe, when do you leave?"

"As soon as the worst of the winter is over," Joe Larribee said. "I'm going to make a trip up there in a week or so and look for a good spot to build my trading post."

Scotty's sleepiness vanished as he realized what they were saying. "You mean you're going to move?" he asked.

"Yes, to the new agency at Pine Ridge. Red Cloud and his people will be settled there this spring, so that's where most of my business will be—Dakota Territory," said Long Joe.

So Sally would be gone, come spring. There was no reason for any regrets; Scotty, too, planned to leave when the winter was over. He and George were going to sell their holdings, split the profits and go their separate ways.

"What about those Cheyennes?" Cornie asked. "Will they be going to Pine Ridge, too? I heard that Red Cloud asked Captain Wessells to let them come and stay with the Dakotas."

Joe shook his head slowly. "He asked, but I don't think the government paid any attention. I think the Cheyennes are to be sent back to Indian Territory within a week or two."

Sally came into the room with a tray of fruit and sweets, and then the children came tumbling in, their cheeks bright red from the cold. Scotty romped with them for a while. Near evening he decided that he would have to go back to the ranch and check the cattle. He hated to leave the warmth and life of the Utterback cabin. Some day he would have a big family like that, and there would be none of the Scottish strictness and reserve with which he had been raised. He told each child goodbye, fishing a piece of Christmas candy out of his deep pocket for every one.

A week later Scotty was back at the fort to collect his pay for the dispatches he had carried during December. He stayed late, talking with friends at the post, and it was well after dark when he started toward the stable to get his horse.

He deliberately walked past the barracks where the fugitive Cheyennes were being housed. The talk at the post now was that they were definitely to be sent back, and they had been told so. Dull Knife's answer was that his people would rather have the soldiers kill them than die of disease and hunger in the south.

So now, Scotty had heard, they sat in the barracks, refusing to budge. Captain Wessells responded by cutting off their food and firewood, then even their drinking water. Still they would not leave.

The cold was biting. The thermometer outside the post supply office read thirty below zero as Scotty walked by. Each breath was painful in his lungs; he was glad he had only a short ride home and the coals of a fire waiting.

The barracks where the Cheyennes were being held was locked. Scotty saw the large padlock and chain on the door, the guard outside stamping his feet to keep warm. There was no smoke coming out of the roof.

"How long are they going to be kept in there?" Scotty asked the guard. "Are they really not being given any food at all?"

"Not a bit. Wessells thinks they'll give up after a few days, but I don't. I'm just glad my shift is only two hours—it's so blasted cold, and sometimes you can hear the kids crying in there."

Scotty heard a scratching sound and saw a hand moving on the window near where they were standing. "What's that?" he asked. "What are they doing?"

"Scraping the frost from the window. They're using it for water."

Back in his warm dugout that night, with the wind howling outside, Scotty kept seeing that thin hand scraping, scraping the window.

He tried to forget the Cheyennes in the following days, working to keep his cattle in sheltered places and see that they were fed. But after another week at the dugout, he was hungry for

news and companionship again, so he rode back to Camp Robinson. He would see if there were any messages to be carried, pick
up the papers, and find out what was going on.

The deadlock had not been broken. This was January 9, and
the Cheyennes had been locked up since the third. This meant
that a hundred and fifty people had spent six days in that un-
heated barracks, with the temperatures still below zero, no food
and no water.

But today there was some hope that things might change. A
council had been called, and two of the Cheyenne leaders—Old
Crow and Wild Hog—were meeting with Captain Wessells.
The Indians refused to send Dull Knife, as they had been told to
do, because they would not trust the *wasichus* with their most respected chief.

Late in the morning Scotty rode to Utterback's. Cornie had returned from a freighting trip the day before and was setting up a
new pot-bellied stove for Zoe that he had brought back from Fort
Pierre.

"Look, it's even got an oven at the side, for baking," he said
proudly as Scotty came in. "Now if I can just get the chimney
vented through the roof—hold this, will you?"

They worked together until the shiny new stove was ready to
use. Zoe watched suspiciously; Scotty could see that the contrap-
tion would have to prove itself to her. She took a pot of coffee
from the fireplace, where she had always done her cooking, and
poured a cup for each of them.

"You think this council that's going on will come to some kind
of settlement for the Cheyennes?" Scotty asked.

Cornie shook his head. "The settlement's already been made.
They're to go back. Wessells is just waiting for them to get too
weak to resist. He doesn't want any black marks on his record. A
careful man, but I think he's misjudged the Cheyennes."

"Why, what can they do?"

"Starve to death. Freeze. Or maybe die fighting."

"Fighting? With what?"

"Oh, they've got weapons. A few old rifles hid under the floorboards in there. Some knives."

"But surely they wouldn't try anything. They're in the middle of a fort full of soldiers, and hungry and cold as they are . . ."

"That's just it. They're desperate."

Scotty looked at his friend curiously. "How do you know so much about the Cheyennes? Nobody's been in or out of that building since it was locked up, except the guards."

"Oh, I wouldn't say that. Zoe and Sally have been pretty busy smuggling in food, and Long Joe even got some firewood to 'em once." He waved a hand at Zoe's warning frown. "It's all right, Scotty isn't the kind who'd tell."

"But how do they get the things in?" Scotty asked.

"There's one guard who's willing to look the other way. It hasn't been much, you understand—just enough to give them a little hope. They divide all the food among the children, and even then it's not . . ."

Cornie was interrupted by a banging on the door. Zoe opened it and her father stepped in, breathing hard and clapping his chapped hands together. "Wessells did it," he said. "Put Old Crow and Wild Hog in irons when they wouldn't agree to go south."

Long Joe had been one of the interpreters at the council. His face blazed with anger, and he did not even seem to notice Scotty. "They weren't interested in hearing what the Cheyennes had to say. All they wanted was to get this so-called 'Indian war' settled so they can look like heroes. When the chiefs wouldn't go along, Wessells put them under arrest."

"So what will Dull Knife do now, I wonder?" Cornie asked.

Long Joe did not answer. He stood looking moodily out of the small window, then buttoned his coat and left without another word. It was growing dark. Cornie invited Scotty to spend the night; Scotty agreed, since he was not ready to go back to the isolation of the ranch. He felt sure that something was going to happen soon.

Zoe cooked supper over the fireplace, ignoring the new stove which stood cold and gleaming in the corner. Cornie seemed to have forgotten all about it and had made no move to fill it with firewood.

They had just gone to bed when Scotty heard the first shot. He sat up on the straw mattress Zoe had fixed for him near the fire. There were more shots, the reports carrying distinctly through the cold night air.

"Something's going on at the fort," Cornie said, padding across the floor to Scotty's bedroll in his bare feet.

"Let's go," said Scotty.

As they pulled on their clothes and boots, the sounds grew louder. Scotty could hear shouts and cries. He buttoned his coat hastily and followed Cornie out the door.

The parade ground in front of the barracks was filled with running figures. When they got close Scotty could see that the door to the building where the Cheyennes had been kept was wide open. The windows, too, had been forced. At first Scotty saw only soldiers racing across the grounds, most of them half dressed, some in their underwear. Then he saw the Indians running toward the open land.

A few had already stopped running. He passed the body of a young boy, perhaps twelve years old, with a large bullet hole in his forehead. A mother was huddled against the wall of the supply room, cradling her child in her arms and moaning.

Scotty had already lost sight of Cornie in the confusion. He went to the woman to see whether he could help her, and was shocked when she pulled away, shielding her face with her arms. He saw the knife in one hand, and pulled back, whispering the Dakota word *"Kola! Kola!"*—friend. He could not think of a single word of Cheyenne, but she seemed to understand and lowered the knife.

"Let's get 'em!" A drifter Scotty had seen hanging around the fort rushed up shouting, his face contorted and his rifle smoking. He saw the woman and swung blindly toward her. Scotty stood up between them, placing his full bulk between the gun and the woman.

The white man wavered. "It's a woman and a child," Scotty said angrily. "Go on."

"Those dirty savages have made enough trouble," the man muttered, and raced away toward the heaviest sound of shooting.

Scotty turned back to the pair by the wall. The woman was thin and haggard, her face deeply lined. Her child, a girl, held her upper left arm with her right hand. Blood was seeping between the fingers. Scotty moved to pick her up, but the mother would not let go.

"Help me get them back to the trading post." Sally Larribee was beside him, whispering. She spoke a few words to the Cheyenne woman and lifted her to her feet. Scotty followed closely, supporting the woman with his arm and covering them from the danger of stray bullets.

It seemed to take hours to cover the short distance to Long Joe's house. Scotty looked at Sally just once and saw that her face was streaked with tears.

On the way they saw an emaciated old Indian man kneeling on the ground, singing.

"What in the world is he singing?" Scotty asked as they drew near.

"His death song," said Sally.

The man's face was calm, and his voice surprisingly strong. He paused for breath, and Sally spoke to him. At first he shook his head, but she persisted, and finally he got to his feet and shuffled along with them, still singing.

Somehow they got the three Cheyennes inside the trading post. Sally's stepmother helped take them to the back, where the family lived. She got some clean clothes and tore them up for bandages, while the Cheyenne mother and child looked on and the man continued singing his death song.

While her stepmother prepared medical help, Sally brought food: bread, dried meat and a dish of pudding.

"I'm going back," Scotty said after a few moments.

Sally followed him back into the empty store. "There's a lot of shooting going on," she said. "Be careful."

"Does it matter to you?"

She looked away in the Indian fashion of reserve. "Yes."

The cold air struck him like a slap in the face when he left the warmth of the store. The shooting was farther away now, and the parade ground was almost deserted. Scotty ran toward the bluffs that showed vaguely in the moonlight ahead. The snow was trampled and marked with blood.

He saw a group of soldiers coming back toward the fort with six or seven prisoners. Behind them came a wagon heaped with bodies. Scotty turned away, sick.

The soldiers seemed to be trying not to shed any more blood. Some of them looked as miserable and angry as Scotty felt. He had heard them talking around the post during the last few weeks, and he knew that many of them were sympathetic toward the Cheyennes. But now other whites were hot on the trail; civilians had come in from the settlement and the nearby ranches at the sound of trouble. They were pursuing the Indians with zest, and he saw some of them leaving the scene with ancient rifles, ragged blankets and other souvenirs.

The rest of the night was a blur. Scotty did what he could, finding the wounded and getting them back to the post hospital. The two miles between the fort and the bluffs were strewn with dead and injured people. But the soldiers told Scotty that some of the escaping Cheyennes had made it to the sheltering hills, and orders were that they would have to be captured and brought back.

By midmorning Scotty and the others had been over the path to the bluffs many times, and there was no sign of any more Indians in the area. Some time during the night he had borrowed a saddle horse from the army stable. He turned its head back toward Camp Robinson and let it carry him over the snow-packed trail.

He was numb, almost numb enough to stop thinking about what was happening. Yet even when he closed his eyes the scene would not go away. This was the adventure he had come to the west to find; this was the great battle that would probably be reported in the newspapers tomorrow as a defeat of the treacherous, hostile Indians.

Scotty had always prided himself on being a realist. Now he wished that he did not see so clearly what was happening and what would continue to happen. Finally, in his exhaustion, all thought and emotion converged into a feeling of total frustration. He was helpless. Something slipped out of his life that night, a sort of confidence in human goodness and happy endings.

It was almost dawn. Scotty returned the horse and let himself into Cornie's house again, trying to be quiet. But he stumbled against a chair in the half-light, and one of the children came padding barefoot across the floor to see who was there. She smiled and held out her arms to him. As he carried her back to bed, he knew he was not ready to give up yet.

8

Strong On January 21, 1879, the last of the Cheyennes
Teeth were brought back to Camp Robinson. Scotty saw
them come in with the soldiers: seven women and children, all
but two badly wounded, and twenty-four bodies.

They had been found hiding in a washout near the head of
Warbonnet Creek and had fought to the last man. Only Dull
Knife himself was still at large, and none of the Indians would say
what had become of him.

Scotty watched the sad procession from the porch of Long
Joe's store. He was getting ready for a freighting trip to the Black
Hills, the last one he would make before his partnership with
George Clark was dissolved. The merchandise was stacked beside
him, ready to be loaded into his wagon. He was only planning to
go as far as Rapid City, and even that was chancy at this time of
year.

When the Indians had been taken to the hospital for treatment
of their wounds and frozen limbs, he went back into the store. It
was almost bare, now, for Long Joe was getting ready to move.
Scotty knocked on the door that led to the Larribee's living quarters, and Sally answered.

"I want to talk to you," he said.

She looked at him with surprise, then came out and closed the door behind her. She sat beside him on the only piece of furniture in the room, a huge old bench with broken legs.

"I'm leaving for Rapid City in the morning," he began. "When I come back, George is going to make one more trip, and then this spring we're going to settle up . . ."

"And you're going back to Kansas," Sally said.

"No, I'm not. That's what I wanted to tell you. I'm going to stay here."

"Why, what made you change your mind?"

Scotty· had never been much of a talker, and it was hard for him now to find words to express the thing that had happened to him. "I've seen this place destroyed," he said, "the buffalo killed off, the open land cut up, trees chopped down, railroads and tele-graph wires strung across it. I guess I've been part of all that. The old way of life that was here is gone, and I can't bring it back. But maybe I could help build something good in its place."

Sally watched him out of the corners of her eyes, silently.

"This could still be a beautiful land," he went on. "There's plenty of room for all of us, Indians and whites, and I think we could make a new life."

"There may be room now," Sally said, "but your people haven't stopped coming. Some day they'll crowd us out of here, and the same thing that happened to the Cheyennes will happen to all of us."

"No. Not if the people who live here can stand up together against it. That's another reason I want to stay. But the most im-portant reason is—well, I want to marry you."

She looked away. "You know what they call a white man with an Indian wife. You want to be a squawman?"

"I want to be your man; that's all."

"I don't know, I'll have to think. I was married before, and he left. Someday you'd want to do that, too, and I don't want that kind of hurt again." Sally spoke slowly and quietly, her accent making it difficult for him to catch each word.

"That much I can promise you; I won't leave," he said.

Sally Philip in later life.

She studied his face. "That's a big promise. Think about it on your way to the hills. If you still mean it when you get back . . . then you can talk to my father."

Scotty tried to examine his own feelings and motives as he struggled to keep the wagon moving over the icy road to Rapid City. He did not think this was a sudden impulse, born of the disgust and shame he felt because of the way the Indians had been treated. He realized now that he had wanted Sally all along, but he had not been ready to give up his freedom.

Now he felt himself part of this new country. He was attracted by the philosophy and the way of life of the Indian people, too. He knew he could never fully understand them, much less become one of them. His mind had been shaped in cold mountains across the ocean, and he could not become a child again. But he could appreciate; he could listen and change as much as he was capable of changing. And it might be that he would have something to offer them, as they tried to make the best of the future that was being forced upon them.

Bad weather hit Rapid City the day Scotty arrived. What had been intended as a short trip turned into a month-long stay since he had to wait for the roads to become passable again.

Cornie Utterback had told Scotty about his own marriage to Zoe Larribee, according to Indian custom. He had first taken gifts to Long Joe, and then he had asked for permission to take Zoe as his wife. Long Joe had agreed and had given a feast on the appointed day for all the family's relatives and friends. There was no formal ceremony—only acceptance by the family and the community that a marriage had taken place.

Scotty had wondered whether he ought to try to bring a minister to Camp Robinson to perform the wedding. But it would probably not mean as much to Sally as the Indian-style marriage. Also, he had observed that marriages among the Dakotas and Cheyennes were taken seriously and usually lasted a lifetime.

So he used the time in Rapid City buying gifts for Long Joe. He picked equipment and trade goods for the Larribee's new store at Pine Ridge and also something personal for each member of the family. For Sally he bought a wedding band.

Scotty made one more trip before he spoke to Long Joe. After delivering his freight and settling up with George Clark, he rode to Red Cloud's camp and the new Pine Ridge agency in Dakota Territory. He knew that Sally would not want to be too far from her family, for her ties with her father, her sisters, her half-brothers and cousins, aunts and uncles were very strong. Scotty had no desire to spend another winter in the crude dugout near Camp Robinson, especially now that the agency had been moved and the old fort almost disbanded.

Following the winding path of White Clay Creek, Scotty rode north until he came to a spot sheltered on three sides by low hills. There was plenty of grass, and the creek nearby for water, and good pasture with draws and breaks where cattle could get out of the wind.

He rode to the top of one of the hills and looked out over the rolling grassland. He could see for miles. Clouds swirled over the horizon, their shapes blending and changing. Sally would like it here; it was a good place.

When he got back to Camp Robinson, Scotty gave his gifts, and the marriage feast was held. Long Joe's Dakota relatives filled his house, and some of Scotty's friends attended too. Most of the soldiers and scouts he had known at Camp Robinson were gone, now that the "Cheyenne trouble" was over and the agency had been moved. But George Clark came, and Cornie Utterback, and Mike Dunn, who had lately married another of the Larribee girls.

Scotty had a chance that day to talk with many of Sally's Indian relatives, and he found his Dakota was improving enough to use it in conversation. Most of them seemed to accept him, now, though he could still feel hostility from a few.

Listening to the Dakotas talk and joke together, Scotty realized again what a false picture most whites had of the Indians. They were nothing like the stern, cold-blooded killers that he had once imagined.

Starting on his third plate of food, Scotty asked one of the women: "What kind of meat is this? It's delicious!"

"Porcupine," she said.

He thought he had misunderstood. Surely he had forgotten the Dakota word. He turned to Sally. "Did she say *porcupine?*"

She nodded. "You've never eaten it before?"

"Oh, yes I have!" Scotty sat down beside the fire and stared at his plate. "I ate some once. And it didn't taste a thing like this. It was the most awful, sickening, stinking stuff . . ." He was speaking in English, but the Indians around the fire seemed to get the meaning from his expression. They began to chuckle, and Sally laughed out loud.

"How did you cook it?" she asked.

"Well, I roasted it over a fire. It was so salty I could hardly stand it, and too tough to chew."

"You have to soak porcupine for days, to get the salty taste out," Sally explained. "And then it has to be cooked slowly, until it's tender, like this. Indians consider it quite a delicacy. But how did you happen to be eating porcupine?"

By now everyone at the feast was listening. Scotty launched into the story of his duel with the porcupine, Sally helping him with the Dakota words occasionally. Everyone laughed uproariously at the thought of Scotty pushing a porcupine out of a tree and then trying to eat it fresh-roasted. One of the old men suggested that Scotty be given a new Indian name: "Strong Teeth."

Sharing the last of the wedding feast with the guests, Scotty thought of the young man he had been just three years ago, hiding in the Black Hills from "wild Indians." Now, at least by marriage, he was a Dakota himself.

9

Plenty   After the wedding Long Joe, Cornie and some of
Horses   the other men went with Scotty to the spot he had
selected on White Clay Creek and helped him build a small
cabin. It had two rooms and a loft, with a large fireplace and a
roof high enough so that Scotty could stand up straight inside. He
had gotten tired of creeping about the dugout with his head down
and his shoulders hunched. They cut the door higher and wider
than usual, too, so that he could get through without so much
trouble.

Scotty used what was left of his savings to buy a few head of
cattle, a sturdy wagon, and a team of mules. He intended to com-
bine cattle raising and freighting, for a few years at least.

He and Sally had been living in the cabin for two weeks when
Agent McGillycuddy paid them a visit. Valentine McGillycuddy, known to the Indians as *Putin Hi Chikala,* or "Little
Whiskers," had been post surgeon at Camp Robinson for a while
and was now the Indian agent at Pine Ridge.

Scotty was working on the small stable he was building for his
horse, mules, and wagon when McGillycuddy came riding up between two Indian policemen.

"Hello, Mr. Philip." The agent dismounted and handed the
reins to one of the policemen. "I thought I'd come by and see
how you're getting along."

McGillycuddy was a handsome man and had the reputation of being intelligent and a good fighter. But Scotty had never cared for him; he was too stiff and cold. Every inch a military man, he seemed to feel comfortable only when he was in charge of a situation.

"Come in," Scotty said. "I'm sure my wife can make us some coffee."

The agent followed him inside and nodded politely to Sally. "This is very nice," he said. "It looks like you're settled in for quite a while."

Scotty set out a chair for McGillycuddy without answering.

"You know," McGillycuddy went on, "a man in your position could do a lot to help with these Indians. Some of them are already friendly and ready to start a new life; but there are others . . ."

"What is it that you want to accomplish with the Dakotas?" Scotty asked.

"Why, we want to get them ready to take their place in society. Education, that's the key. If we can get the children away from the influence of the old ways, teach them something better, then in a few years . . ."

"They'll be just like us?"

"More or less. Of course, it will take time. Some of these Easterners seem to think we can make these roving bands of hunters into small farmers within a year or two. It's not going to be that easy."

"I agree with you there," Scotty said. "This isn't farm land anyway. There isn't enough rainfall. But why do we have to try to change the Indians at all? The treaties say they're to have this land, and rations—they don't say the Dakotas have to give up all their traditions."

McGillycuddy looked at him coldly. "You think we should just let these people sit here, being fed by the government forever?"

"Maybe they could go into cattle raising. That would make more sense than farming."

"Nothing will be accomplished here until we get hostiles like Red Cloud under control. That will be my first goal, and I hope you white men living on the reservation will cooperate. You could do a lot, for instance, to help persuade parents to send their children to school."

"You're setting up a school here at Pine Ridge?"

"Yes. And I also had a letter from a new Indian school that's being started in Carlisle, Pennsylvania. The headmaster is coming this summer to recruit students."

"Why would they want to take children away from their families, all the way to Pennsylvania?"

"This school will be especially designed for Indians, to help them learn our way of life. The people who are building it believe that the children must be taken out of their old environment, forced to use English, disciplined properly, and dressed appropriately. The boys will have their hair cut, and all will learn useful skills . . ."

Scotty shifted his weight in the hard chair. "I just can't see what will be accomplished by blotting out everything that's important to these children."

McGillycuddy was on his feet, glaring at Scotty. "Just remember, Philip, I have the power to ban anyone from this agency. Don't try to get in the way of progress." He stalked to the door and was gone with a crash and a clatter of hooves.

Sally looked after him and shrugged, then picked up the empty coffee cups.

Through that summer Scotty was too busy to worry about the agent's threats. He made freighting trips to Fort Pierre and the

Black Hills, hiring two young Dakotas to watch his cattle. While he was away Sally went down to Pine Ridge to visit her family, so she always kept him up to date on the news. McGillyguddy was feuding openly with Red Cloud, and also with army officers and Interior Department officials—anyone, it seemed, who disagreed about what was best for his charges.

Yet there were times when McGillycuddy was more in touch with reality than some of the Eastern bureaucrats who wanted to make small farmers out of the Dakotas. Sally witnessed one discussion in front of the agent's office in which McGillycuddy told an official to try farming the dry soil of western Dakota Territory himself if he felt it was such a promising idea.

One morning in August Scotty brought his team and wagon back to the ranch after a long freighting trip. Later he would ride down to Pine Ridge to get Sally and Posey, but he wanted to take a nap and clean up first. He had been away for almost two weeks. The prices for his freight had not been as good as he expected, the wagon had broken down, and one night he had been forced to sleep outside in the pouring rain. The weather was still damp and cool, unusual for August.

He got down from the wagon and winced, his stiff muscles aching with every step. As he reached out to open the door, he noticed that it was just slightly ajar. At the same time, he looked around and saw footprints in the still-soft mud around the house. Someone had been here recently, or was inside now.

Scotty was more curious than alarmed. He had fixed a crude lock on the door for the times when he had to be away for many days, but it would not be difficult to jar loose. People on the reservation expected guests to come walking in at any time, and all the cabins were considered open to a traveler who needed a place to stay.

After wiping his boots rather loudly on the doorstep, Scotty walked in and saw a pair of bare legs dangling from the window. He grabbed the wiggling brown legs, and in a few moments had pulled a young Indian boy back into the room. The boy struggled against Scotty's grasp and then stood glaring sullenly.

He looked about ten years old. Dressed only in a torn shirt and breech cloth, he was thin and small to be so fierce. His legs were scratched, and the moccasins on his feet were falling apart.

"*How kola,*" Scotty said, but the boy did not respond to the friendly greeting. Scotty questioned him as kindly as he could. All he could find out was that the boy's name was Plenty Horses, and he was afraid Scotty would turn him over to the police or the *wasichus*.

Finally Scotty coaxed until the boy blurted two English words: "school," and "Carlisle." Then Scotty understood.

Captain Pratt, the headmaster of the new Indian school in Pennysylvania, had visited both the Rosebud and Pine Ridge reservations recently, seeking students for the fall term. Some parents had been persuaded to agree to send their children. The methods of persuasion had ranged from extolling the values of education to threatening to cut down on rations, and some eighty-four pupils had been recruited. Now some of the parents and many of the children were having second thoughts about the whole thing.

Scotty brought in what food supplies he had left on the wagon and cooked a meal. Plenty Horses ate hungrily, though he still watched Scotty with distrust. At last the boy lay down beside the fire and drifted off to sleep.

He looked very young, lying there. Scotty remembered how he had loved to curl up beside the big fireplace in the Philip home in Morayshire as a boy. When winter came, he and Sally would have a child of their own. Plenty Horses made him think of his own unborn baby, too, and of the future.

Scotty washed, shaved, trimmed his moustache and changed to clean clothes. In all that time the Indian boy did not move. Scotty left food and water near the fireplace, went out, and closed the door quietly behind him.

He took the small buckboard, which slowed him down on the trip to the agency. Alone on horseback, he could have made the journey in an hour, but it was nearly evening by the time he got back to the ranch.

He did not tell Sally about Plenty Horses until they were on the way home. She recognized the name; the boy was one of the Brule band of Dakotas. She had heard that he and several other Brule boys had run away from their families rather than be sent to Carlisle.

"What do you think? Should we take him back to his father and mother?" Scotty asked.

"I don't know," said Sally. "They don't want him to go to that school, either, but they agreed to it before and now the agent says he has to go."

"Maybe education is the right thing," Scotty said, "but I don't see why it has to be so far away. School is bad enough even when you can go home at night."

"You didn't like school?" Sally looked at him with surprise.

"I hated it." Scotty remembered vividly the little stone building, the seats that were always too small, the schoolmaster rapping his hands with a ruler or beating him with a cane.

"But why do you have all those books? Why do you read so much?"

"Books are one thing, school's another. Still, I suppose I couldn't enjoy reading if I hadn't been taught. I don't know what the answer is. If the Dakotas are going to hold onto their rights and become self-supporting, they'll have to learn to communicate with the whites—to speak English, read, and so forth. But I hate to see these children being practically kidnapped."

When they got home Plenty Horses was gone. Scotty had not really expected him to stay; he had recognized the look in the boy's eyes.

A few days later Zoe came to visit, and she told them that the Indian police had found the young Brule and put him on the train to Carlisle.

In the fall Scotty rode out with his two Indian helpers to round up his small herd of cattle and decide which animals should be sold before winter. They had to ride many miles over the prairie, separating so as to cover more distance.

One evening late in September Scotty made camp alone in a draw beside a tiny creek. He was on his way back to the ranch with two cows and their calves. Near his camp, on the other side of the creek, was the skeleton of a large buffalo. Wolves had picked the carcass clean and scattered the bones, but hidden here in the draw they had not been picked up by the men who sold buffalo bones for fertilizer.

Scotty heard the approaching horses long before they came upon him and his fire. It was not dark yet, and he could see the six young Indians riding toward him along the creek bed. He called to them and offered to share his food and coffee.

The six were from the Cheyenne River agency to the north. They told Scotty they had been visiting at Pine Ridge and were on their way home. Scotty watched them as they ate; they were tremendously excited about something. Their eyes gleamed, and they could not sit still.

"You bring good news?" Scotty finally asked them, in Dakota.

They all nodded and looked at each other. Scotty sensed them deciding, without words, whether he could be trusted or not. Then one of them smiled and said, with wonder in his voice:

"The buffalo are coming! They are coming back to us."

10

Twice Married For a few days the wonderful news seemed to be true—at least to the Dakotas who wanted so desperately to believe it. The men rode away from the reservations, with or without their agents' permission, and came back loaded down with meat and skins. It was like the old days.

Some of Sally's Dakota relatives came to invite them to a feast. Scotty, Sally, and Posey rode in the buckboard to the log cabin camp near the agency and stayed overnight.

The Indians' joy was infectious. The bad times were forgotten: there was plenty to eat now, and everyone shared the feast. A great kettle of succulent buffalo stew bubbled over the fire. There was dancing and singing and much joking.

Sally's uncle, an old man named One Eye, came to where Scotty was sitting in a corner of the cabin and offered him another bowl of stew.

"Such a big man must need much food," he said in Dakota.

"Thank you," said Scotty, knowing better than to refuse, though he had already eaten too much.

"The buffalo have come back to us. Now we can all be happy again," the old man said.

"But what if they vanish again?" As soon as the words were out of his mouth, Scotty knew he should not have spoken. He bit his tongue angrily; he had meant to keep his opinions to himself tonight.

"The buffalo have come back to us."

One Eye's happy expression became serious. "Then we will die," he said.

Scotty knew that most of the Indian leaders and the younger warriors were aware of the truth. The buffalo had not come back.

This had just been one small remnant of the onetime northern herd. Escaping somehow from the professional hunters, the few remaining buffalo had run east. Now they, too, had been killed.

Soon after the feast the weather turned wintry, and there was no more traveling for a while. Scotty stayed close to the ranch. In December he brought Zoe up from Pine Ridge, where Cornie was freighting rations. She was there to help when Mary Philip was born.

Looking at his daughter for the first time, Scotty felt very strange. She seemed unbelievably small and delicate, and he noticed the worry on Zoe's face as she held the baby.

"Zoe," he whispered, for Sally was sleeping in the next room, "is there something wrong with her?"

"No, no, it's not that. But she isn't a strong baby. She's so tiny, even her crying is soft. We'll just hope . . ."

Sally recovered quickly, and the baby, too, seemed to be doing better. After Zoe had gone home, Scotty tried to help Sally with the heavy chores and keep some of Posey's time occupied. The little boy did not seem to resent his new sister, but he missed the full attention of his mother. Scotty did not hold the baby until she was a month old, and even then she seemed lost in the curve of his big arm.

In the spring Scotty set out for the Black Hills again. He delivered a load of rations to the Cheyenne River agency and was heading west with a load consigned for Rapid City when he noticed a herd of cattle grazing beside the bank of a river. It was not really the cattle that caught his eye, but five buffalo calves that moved peacefully among the Herefords.

At first he thought his eyes were playing tricks on him, but when he rode closer he saw that they really were buffalo calves. He was watching them curiously when a man came riding up over a nearby hill and stopped beside Scotty's wagon.

"You looking for cattle?" The man was tall and thin, with light brown skin and thick black hair. Scotty thought he was at least half Indian, though he was dressed like a white cowboy.

"My name's Scotty Philip; I've got a ranch down by Pine Ridge. I was just wondering about those buffalo calves in with your herd."

"Oh! Well, I'm Pete Dupree. Caught those calves at the hunt last fall. I brought 'em back here to see how they'd do with the cattle."

"You planning to keep them and raise them?"

"Don't know. Just seems a shame to see the last of the buffalo gone. I might keep these awhile, if they're not too much trouble. I still like the meat better than beef."

Pete Dupree invited Scotty to spend the night, as was the custom in this empty land. After a hot supper they talked about the economics of fattening and selling beef cattle. Pete's cabin was hardly big enough for himself, his wife and children, but they found a place for Scotty to put his bedroll for the night. He was off for the Black Hills early the next morning.

The freighting trips were becoming more and more tiresome. Scotty disliked leaving Sally alone with the children, and he hated the long, weary trail from Pierre to the Black Hills and back. In his hotel room in Rapid City, he counted the profits of the trip and mentally added his savings—there would be enough to buy some new stock soon. Maybe by this summer he could give up freighting and spend all his time raising cattle.

He got to the ranch a week later, at about noon one mild April day. There was a strange rig outside, and a brown mare was tied to the fence. The front door opened as Scotty was unhitching his team—and George Philip came out, followed by Sally and Posey.

"Geordie!" Scotty grabbed his brother's hand and tried to say something more, but surprise made his mind go blank.

"Good to see you, Jamie, lad." George put a hand on Scotty's shoulder.

"But what are you doing here? How did you find me?"

"Well, now, we hadn't heard from you for so long and we just wanted to know what you were doing up here. I did have a time tracking you down: went first to Camp Robinson, then to the Pine Ridge agency, and they sent me up here."

"I guess I haven't written for a long time. I've been busy . . ." Scotty broke off, not knowing what more to say. It was true that he had not written to his family for two years, since before his marriage. He was not ashamed of Sally, but he had not been sure what the Philips would think of his staying in Dakota Territory with an Indian wife. He glanced at Sally; she did not seem upset. Nor did George, who was beaming through his bushy brown beard. "How long have you been here?" Scotty asked.

"Oh, just since this morning."

George stayed a week, and in that time he brought Scotty up to date on all the family news. David was still in Canada, and Alex had started his own farm near Hays, Kansas. Robert Philip, a favorite brother of Scotty's, had died back in Scotland, leaving his wife with a baby boy to care for. George now had a store in Hays, and the Victoria colony had been disbanded.

One afternoon Scotty took his brother out on horseback to show him some of the countryside.

"How much of this is your land?" George asked as they loped along the creek bank.

"None of it—or all of it. This is the Dakota Indian reservation, you know. It's owned by the tribe. I'm allowed to run cattle on it because Sally's a member of the tribe. Actually, by Dakota law I belong to the Dakotas, too, as her husband."

"But is there any security in this? If you don't own the land . . ."

"I don't need to own it. This isn't farm land, George, in spite of what the Interior Department is trying to tell the Indians. It's good for cattle raising; the grass makes wonderful feed."

"You don't intend coming back to Kansas, then?"

"No." Scotty shifted in the saddle and turned to look at his brother. "I like it here. Besides, Sally would never be happy anywhere else."

"She told me you were married back at Camp Robinson, a year and a half ago. But there was no minister or judge or anyone like that?"

Scotty struggled to control his rising temper. "We were married in the Indian way, by their laws. I consider it perfectly binding; she's my wife."

"Jamie, think about her. What if something happened to you? Is there a legal record of your marriage? Would she be able to inherit your property, take care of the children?"

"I told you, we're married by Dakota law. That's good enough." Scotty had always resented the way his older brother tried to run his life. In the old days it had seemed that nothing Scotty decided to do was ever quite right; George always had to point out his mistakes.

By the time George left to go back to Kansas, Scotty's anger had cooled and he had to admit to himself that George might be right. The old Indian ways were already disappearing; ten or twenty years from now his marriage might seem nothing more than a common law arrangement. Still, he would feel rather foolish going to get married with two children along. Three, if he waited many more months, for Sally was expecting another child.

Baby Mary still seemed terribly frail and listless. Sometimes, holding her, Scotty thought that she was not very interested in life; she slept too much, and moved too feebly.

A spring cold which started during a spell of cool, rainy weather would not leave the child. She coughed in the night, her little voice high and thin. Sally walked the floor with her or sat rocking her in front of the fire, but nothing seemed to help. The cough became a sort of wheeze deep in the baby's chest. Scotty brought the doctor out from the agency to look at her, and he left some medicine to be spoon-fed to her. The doctor was very quiet on the way back to Pine Ridge; Scotty sensed that he did not want to say what he really thought.

One morning two days later Scotty woke to singing. It was Sally, crooning in Dakota. He knew what had happened the moment he saw her tear-stained face. She had found the baby dead that morning, and she was singing her grief in the Indian way.

Mary looked peaceful in her little bed. There was no sign of suffering, only the sweet expression of a tired child sleeping.

Scotty put a hand on Sally's shoulder for a moment, then went outside. He looked blindly at the rising sun. He did not know what to do; he could not cry. Ever since he had been a little boy it had been drummed into him that men do not cry. He stood listening to the wailing notes of Sally's song.

Grief was expressed very openly by the Indians, Scotty knew. He had gone to visit some of his Dakota neighbors after a death in the family, and had seen both men and women cry, tear their clothes and even slash their own flesh. At first Scotty had been uncomfortable, believing as he always had that a brave person did not show his feelings. But he had noticed that Indian people did not turn bitter or morbid after a death, as whites often did. They expressed suffering and then put it behind them, not to be forgotten but to be cherished as an important part of the past.

Scotty went to his tool shed and got some smooth boards that he had brought from Pierre to use in building furniture during the long winter months. Blindly, moving like a puppet, he made a small, narrow box.

Late in the afternoon Sally's family began to arrive. Scotty never knew how they learned of the baby's death; perhaps someone had stopped in during the morning while Scotty was working in the shed. He watched them driving up in wagons or coming on horseback: Zoe and Cornie, One Eye and his family, Long Joe Larribee, and many others. They brought food, and it was shared. Voices joined Sally's in singing the Dakota songs of death and grieving.

Scotty stayed outside, alone. He could not join in the emotional outpouring, and he knew the Indians would consider him very strange if he did not. Children were their most precious possessions, and to them the death of a child was the greatest possible tragedy. Somehow the very sound of their grieving comforted Scotty. As he listened, tending the animals in the barn, he felt a sort of release of his own choking misery.

Later he was able to talk with them a little. The Indian people offered no false or easy words of comfort. But they made Scotty feel that sorrow, like good fortune, could be shared—and that made it bearable.

After Mary's death Scotty became restless. The ranch did not suit him any more; there was not enough water for the number of cattle he wanted to run, and the area was becoming crowded as small groups of Dakotas built their log cabins around the agency. The government was still pushing its program of small farming for the Indians, and some of them were trying to comply. Cattle and farms did not mix. So Scotty began looking for a new base, farther from Pine Ridge.

He finally settled on a spot on the Bad River, about half-way between the Pine Ridge and Cheyenne River agencies. The country was still open here; though Indians passed constantly on their way to visit from one agency to the other, few of them actually lived in the area. This was an advantage for the large cattle operation Scotty had in mind, but it made for a rather lonely life at first.

The new baby, Amy, was born before they made the move.

From the beginning she was stronger and healthier than Mary. She ate, cried, and played lustily, and Scotty never feared for her in the way he had for the first baby. She helped Sally, too, by giving her a new interest and purpose.

They made the move to the Bad River in midsummer, 1881. Scotty had already built a good-sized house, bought some new stock and even hired three cowboys. It was all a gamble, depending on how well the cattle sold in the fall and again the next spring.

His first year was good. The Texas cattle thrived on the nutritious Dakota grass and went to market fat and sleek. Through the summer Scotty and his hands tried to keep track of their "L-7" brand cattle roaming the unfenced land. There were other ranchers on the two reservations: some Indians, some half-breeds and a few whites, who like Scotty had married Indian women. By custom, each rancher turned the cattle of another man toward their home range, and they all knew each other's brands.

After George's visit, Scotty had often thought about his brother's advice. Finally, on New Year's Day, 1882, he took Sally down to Pine Ridge and asked the Episcopal missionary there, Reverend Robinson, to remarry them. They celebrated with an all-night wedding dance, with the music provided by "Zither Dick" Boesl.

Late in the evening Scotty and Sally went outside to get a drink of cool well water and catch their breath. Scotty drew the water and poured a tin cup full for Sally.

"You feel any different now, Mrs. Philip?" he asked as he handed it to her. "Is twice married better than once?"

She shook her head and smiled. "It didn't change anything for me. But I know you were trying to do the right thing. Nothing is as simple as it was before. Your people and mine are getting farther apart all the time."

Scotty was surprised to hear her speak that way. He studied her face, the shadowed eyes. "You still think of it as 'your people' and 'my people'?" he asked her.

"Yes—and yet I'm not all Indian, and you're not all white any more, either. Sometimes I wonder what we are."

Scotty was quiet for a moment, watching her. He had long ago stopped thinking of her as "Indian": she was Sally. Did she still think of him as a *wasichu?* "Well," he said, "I hope you're not sorry you married me. If you are, you've made the same mistake twice now."

She laughed. "And so have you." Then she went on, her face growing serious again: "I wasn't talking about you and me. What I meant was, there's trouble coming. People say the government men are coming again, wanting more of our land."

"There is talk of another treaty. But according to the Treaty of 1868, they can't make any more agreements with the Dakotas without three-fourths of the men signing." Scotty had tried to become informed on the laws regarding Indian lands and rights since he was technically a Dakota by virtue of his marriage. "This treaty they're talking of now is just to make administration easier . . ."

"I don't know what's in your newspapers," Sally said. "But I know about treaties. I know how the Dakotas feel. Some of them won't even trust me anymore, because I'm not a fullblood and because . . ."

"Because you married me. *Are* you sorry?"

"Not that I married you. Never that. I'm only sorry that your people can't leave us alone. Sometimes I think they won't be satisfied until they've done the same thing to us that they did to the buffalo."

Scotty did not answer.

11

William Temple Hornaday In the fall of 1882 Scotty and his cowhands drove about fifty fat cattle to Fort Pierre to be sold. They stayed in town for several days while Scotty worked out the details of the sale. One evening on the way back to his hotel he picked up a newspaper from Yankton. On the front page, in bold headlines, he read:

LAND TO BE OPENED FOR SETTLEMENT!

Sioux Reservation Being Broken Up
And Sold To U.S. Government

"What's this all about?" Scotty asked the clerk at the hotel, showing him the paper.

"Oh, haven't you heard? They're opening up the reservation land . . ."

"*Who's* opening it up?"

"Why, the government. You know, the Edmunds Commission. Matter of fact, Mr. Edmunds and his committee have just come back from Pine Ridge, and they're staying in this hotel!"

"Could you tell me what room? I'd like to meet Edmunds. I've heard a little about his commission, but what I've heard isn't what I'm reading in this paper."

"Well, he's staying in Room 216 . . ." The clerk hesitated, clearly wondering what this huge cowboy might want with Newton Edmunds. But Scotty was already on his way upstairs.

A well-dressed, smooth-looking man answered his knock.

"My name's Scotty Philip. I have a ranch on the Bad River west of here, and I'm in Pierre selling some of my herd."

"Come in, Mr. Philip, I'm Newton Edmunds. What can I do for you?" The man's professional friendliness irritated Scotty.

"I just wondered whether you'd seen this Yankton newspaper." Scotty stepped inside and showed Edmunds the paper.

"No, I didn't realize the news was out." Edmunds frowned, reading the story quickly. "Someone is in a hurry to start selling the land; this should have waited until we had all the signatures on the treaty."

"But is it true?"

Edmund's face cleared. "Oh, I see, you're concerned about getting in on the sale. Rest assured, Mr. Philip, everyone will have a chance . . ."

"Mr. Edmunds, the Dakotas I've talked to believe that your treaty simply breaks up the reservation into different parts, for the separate Dakota tribes. They don't know that they're selling their land to the government or that it's to be opened for white settlers."

Newton Edmunds studied Scotty, as though he were trying to guess exactly what the interest of a white rancher might be in the land sale. "It's difficult to communicate with those people," he said finally, "and maybe the interpreters aren't doing their jobs. It's all written down in the treaty, Mr. Philip, just as it is here in the paper. They're to get a thousand bulls and twenty-five thousand cows for the land."

"They've been told about the cattle, but not about the land." Scotty figured in his head for a moment. "Let's see, twenty-six thousand head of cattle—that might be worth a million dollars at the current price."

"Yes. A fair amount for a tribe of half-wild Indians who don't need the land anyway, wouldn't you say?"

"Figures out to about eight cents an acre. No, I don't think it's a fair price. And I don't think you'll ever get three-fourths of the men to sign that treaty, either."

"What are you talking about? Of course we won't get three-fourths of the men to sign; that could take years! The chiefs can sign for the tribe as they always have. At Pine Ridge we already got eighty of the important headmen to sign the treaty."

"Out of what—seven thousand? Mr. Edmunds, the treaty of 1868 required that any future agreements with the Dakotas had to be signed by three-fourths of the adult males. The United States government guaranteed that."

Edmunds glared at Scotty and opened the door. "Philip, you strike me as a troublemaker. I don't know what your interest is in this—maybe you just want to keep settlers out of western Dakota. What right do you have to live there, anyway? I suppose you're a half-breed, or a squawman. Well, you people can't keep that land to yourself forever."

Scotty stalked out of the room.

Through the fall and winter Scotty talked to many of the Indians from the different agencies, and the more he heard about the land sale the angrier he became. It was true that the people who had first been approached at Pine Ridge had not understood that they were selling more than half the reservation to the whites. But by this time Scotty and others who could read the newspapers had informed the Dakotas just what was in the proposed treaty. Most of the men at the Rosebud, Cheyenne River, and Standing Rock agencies were now completely opposed to the agreement.

Still, Scotty heard stories of various kinds of pressure being applied to force the Indians to sign. Some were told that rations would be cut off if they did not go along; some even heard the threat that the whole tribe would be moved to Indian Territory, as the northern Cheyennes had been.

One day in the spring of 1883, Long Joe Larribee came to the Philip ranch. He was on his way to Fort Pierre to pick up a load of rations for the Pine Ridge agency, and was full of anger at the manipulations of the treaty commission.

"What gets me," said Scotty, "is the way they've gone about this. Trying to talk a few so-called chiefs into signing for the whole tribe, not even telling some of them what was in the treaty. I honestly think they figured the Indians wouldn't realize what was going on even after they put it in the newspapers."

"They figure because most Indians can't read, they're stupid," Long Joe said.

"I think they'll find out different before this is over." Scotty smiled. "When Edmunds has tangled with Red Cloud, White Thunder, Gall, and some of the others, he'll know he's been in a fight."

"How're you doing with your cattle?" Joe asked as they walked back to the house.

"Pretty well, so far. I'm going down to Texas soon with a couple of men, and I'm going to buy a lot more stock there and drive them back."

"You're getting quite a large operation going, ain't you? How would the land sale affect your business?"

Scotty stopped and looked hard at his father-in-law's dark face. "Do you think I'm against the land sale because I don't want competition?"

Long Joe smiled kindly. "No. But others'll be saying it. You're a good businessman, Scotty; you like to buy and sell and make money. No matter how much sympathy you have for the Indians, you'll never be one of them. And it's hard to be on both sides at once. I know."

On the long trip to Texas and back, Scotty thought about what Larribee had said. It was true; he was not even sure of his own motives any more. He met other cattlemen who wanted to use the grazing land of western Dakota, and he could not blame them for resenting the tribal rights he had gained through his marriage. He liked and admired the Indians. He wanted to see them treated fairly. But what, after all, could one man do to hold back the changes that were coming?

By the time Scotty got back to Dakota, the land sale had fallen through, at least for the time being. Sally told him that some of the missionaries on the reservations had written letters to their denominations back East, exposing what was going on. The churches had joined with Senator Henry Dawes of Massachusetts and other powerful men to pressure the Senate into ending the negotiations.

Still, it was not the idea of the land sale these people opposed, so much as the underhanded way in which it was being pushed. After reading the newspapers, Scotty was convinced that those who wanted Indian land would try again.

Scotty's life in the next few years centered around the ranch and his family. Each summer he added a few more head to the herd, a few more cowhands and another building or two. Each fall he took more healthy cattle to market.

He and Posey were quickly outnumbered by the female side of the family. Tina, Olive, and Hazel were born in the early years on the Bad River. Scotty sometimes wished for a son of his own, but he liked to watch the pretty, laughing girls following their mother around or playing in the yard.

One afternoon in the spring of 1886 Scotty rode out in a rainstorm to check the cattle. For half an hour the thunder rolled like a mountain avalanche, and the nervous animals milled and bellowed their fear. It was all Scotty and his men could do to keep them from running. Then the noise faded, and the storm settled into a steady, drenching rain that looked like it would go on all day. Scotty left three of his cowboys to watch the herd and turned his horse toward home.

He was soaked, and his muscles ached. Rain blew into his face, dripped off his moustache and down his neck. When he first saw the wagon mired in the mud a mile from his ranch, he thought it was empty. Then he noticed a man sitting quietly on a rock, dressed in city clothes and a homburg hat.

"Sir," he called when he saw Scotty, "I wonder if you'd help me pull this wagon out of the mud. I'll be glad to pay . . ."

"You won't get out of that gumbo today," Scotty said. "Not a chance. Better unhitch your horse and ride him over to my ranch."

Scotty waited while the man got the horse free and climbed clumsily onto its bare back. Then Scotty led the way home, skirting the worst mudholes and the deep draws.

It was wonderful to get inside the warm cabin. Sally and the children looked curiously at the visitor, who removed his soggy hat and smiled at them. "My name is William Temple Hornaday," he said.

"Scotty Philip. That's my wife, Sally, and the children: Posey, Amy, Tina, Olive, and the baby, Hazel. There's a bedroom over there, where you can get out of those wet clothes."

"I left my things in the wagon."

Scotty rummaged in a wooden chest in the corner of the kitchen. "Here's a pair of pants and a flannel shirt, both too small for me now. You can wear 'em 'til Sally gets your things dried by the fire."

Scotty changed, too, and a few moments later Hornaday came out of the bedroom. He looked different, and a bit ridiculous, in Scotty's old clothes, which hung on his slim body like a two-layer tent. But Scotty liked his face.

Hornaday picked up the buffalo robe which was draped over a bench near the stove. "This is a beautiful hide," he said. "It's so soft and pliable—did you cure it yourself?"

"No, I bought it from the Indians. Nobody can make a buffalo robe the way they do."

The visitor sat down on the bench, still fingering the robe. "I'm looking for bison, Mr. Philip. Live bison. Can you tell me where I could find some?"

"Live buffalo? Don't you know the herds were all killed off years ago? If it's hunting you're looking for, Hornaday, you'd better go back East and forget it." Scotty was disappointed: he had thought this man was more than just another dude buffalo hunter coming to Dakota fifteen years too late.

"I don't want to hunt bison, er, buffalo. At least, that's not the main idea. I'm the chief taxidermist for the National Museum in Washington, and we want an exhibit of American bison."

"Taxidermist? You mean, you want to *stuff* them?"

"Yes, just a few, for a western exhibit we're working on. The thing is, I've discovered that the bison have been almost entirely killed off."

"Anybody out here could have told you that."

"So I'm finding out. But the American public in general doesn't realize that these animals are on the verge of becoming extinct. I hope when I get back to Washington that I can do something about it."

Scotty caught Tina, who came dashing by, and swooped her up to sit on his shoulder. "What can you do about it?" he asked.

"Why, a law, for the protection of American bison. A law against hunting them, setting aside land where they can live unmolested."

"That would be fine, if there are any left to protect."

Hornaday rolled up the sleeves of Scotty's old shirt so that his hands were free. "Have you got a paper and a pencil?" he asked. "I can tell you almost exactly how many bison are left."

Scotty brought him a scrap of letter paper and a pencil. The taxidermist scribbled thoughtfully, then added his figures. "About two hundred in the Texas panhandle; a few dozen in Montana, north of the Yellowstone, still wild; the Michael Pablo herd in Montana, maybe a hundred; and some in Canada. All told, I'd say there are less than five hundred bison left alive on this continent."

"A bad winter could wipe them out, or disease . . ."

"Or hunters. That's why I want to try to get legislation passed, before they're all dead and gone forever."

Sally came and called them to the table. They warmed their insides with stew and hot cornmeal bread, the children giggling shyly when the stranger tried to talk to them. In the middle of the meal Scotty slammed his coffee cup down on the table and turned to Hornaday.

"I forgot! There are some buffalo left in Dakota, or at least there might be. A rancher up north, what's his name—something French. Dupree, that's it. Pete Dupree. He had some buffalo calves in with his cattle about four years ago."

"That must be the man I'm looking for. Someone down at the Pine Ridge agency told me there was a man in this area with some bison. Can you direct me to him?"

Scotty got more paper and, while Sally cleared the table, drew a map for Hornaday. "This is where he lives, near as I remember.

If you get within a few miles, just ask anyone you see for Pete Dupree."

The rain stopped in the night. Early the next morning Scotty took Mr. Hornaday back to his mired wagon, and in half an hour they had it dug out and pulled free. They shook hands, Scotty feeling a real liking for William Temple Hornaday.

"Tell me," Scotty asked as his new friend climbed onto the wagon seat, "why do you care about the buffalo? You're an easterner, an educated man; what difference does it make to you if they're killed off?"

Hornaday looked puzzled. "Why, because it shouldn't happen, that's all. This is a big country. There ought to be room in it for those who had it first. We have no right to destroy the land and the animals, as though everything that seems to be in our way is worthless. Goodbye, Mr. Philip, and thank you again for your hospitality."

12

Dakota Scotty forgot about Hornaday and his project as
Winter the grinding work of the summer began. July and
August of 1886 were unusually hot and dry. Scotty and his men
rode long miles, getting the cattle to waterholes and watching
them eat the spiky brown grass. Grasshoppers appeared in great
swarms, eating whatever was in sight. Prairie fires, started by
lightning, frightened the cattle and burned off the land. When
the time for marketing came, the herd was in poor condition.

Scotty decided not to sell many of his cattle since they were so
thin and weak. He would hope for a mild winter and a good, wet
spring to fatten them for market.

In October he went to Fort Pierre and borrowed enough
money to pay his cowboys and get supplies for the winter. The
banker there had known Scotty long enough and had done
enough business with him to loan him several thousand dollars
with no security but Scotty's signature on a piece of paper.

The snow began in November, six weeks earlier than usual.
Winds howling out of the northwest drove the snow into huge
drifts, and the mercury dropped to forty below zero, then fifty
below. Storm followed storm. Whenever the weather warmed up
a little, it would snow again.

Scotty did what he could to save his cattle, but that was very little, with his cowhands gone for the winter and the snow so impossibly deep.

He went out on snowshoes one morning in December, pulling bales of prairie hay on a homemade sled behind him. Each breath Scotty took hung on the air like a puff of smoke. The extremely low temperatures had frozen a crust on the top of the snow, and he walked on it without too much difficulty. His neck and face were wrapped in a woolen scarf, and he wore a heavy buffalo-skin coat and leather boots, but the cold still crept in to chill his blood.

He found a few head of his cattle huddled together behind a small hill. They were pitifully thin, and their legs were torn and bleeding. While a man could walk on the hard-crusted snow, the cattle broke through, scraping the skin from their legs and flanks. Normally, they would have been eating the prairie grass, scratching clear patches in the snow with their hooves. But now the grass was buried under several feet of ice and snow, and the only available food was the leaves of willows and cottonwoods along creek beds.

Scotty unloaded some of the baled hay. It was all he could do; there was no shelter he could take the cattle to. They would have to live or die as nature decided.

There was a waterhole nearby, a deep pool in a creek that ran into the Bad River. A dozen of Scotty's cattle were there, sheltered from the worst of the wind by the little draw. He put out more hay for them, and then decided to chop a hole in the ice near the edge of the pool. At least the cattle might get something to drink before it froze over again. Scotty took an axe from the sled and went to work.

He was tired and stiff from the cold. Somehow he slipped, lost his footing and, before he could catch himself, fell through the half-finished hole and into the icy water of the creek.

Get out, get out now, he told himself. You'll freeze in a few minutes in this water, or sink in and drown. He tried to heft his body out and onto the solid ice, but he could not find anything to hold onto. The cattle watched him dumbly, without interest.

Numbness was flowing over his body, easing the intense pain of the first few minutes. Desperately, he plunged first one arm and then the other into the water. Then he laid the wet sleeves of his coat on the ice, pushing down as hard as he could. When he thought they were frozen to the ice, he struggled out of the coat, and holding to it, pulled himself up and out.

Now he had to get home. His clothes were soaking wet, but they would freeze on his body before long. The snowshoes were at the bottom of the creek. He left the sled where it was and forced himself to run against time and the cold. He had seen many men who had lost fingers, hands, or feet to frostbite. Thinking of that, he ran faster, hoping by the motion to keep life in all his flesh.

The longest part of the journey was from the time he saw the house until he stumbled through the door like a grotesque, living snowman. Sally wasted no time asking him what had happened. She brought blankets and helped him get out of his stiff, crackling clothes while he stood in front of the hot stove. Then he climbed into bed, wrapped in all the covers Sally could find. For a long time he lay shivering. Sally made coffee and poured some between his chattering teeth, and at last he drifted into an uneasy sleep.

Scotty stayed close to home for weeks after that. He had escaped without any serious frostbite, but he did not want to take too many chances with the lethal cold. Occasionally the weather eased a little, and he ventured out to feed any cattle he could find. But then more snow would come, and he would stay at home, reading or working around the house and barn. His horses and a few of his best cattle were sheltered there—at least they would survive the winter.

The last big blizzard came at the end of January, 1887. Tem-

peratures warmed gradually through February, and then at last
the spring thaw swelled the rivers and creeks. The melting snow
revealed the corpses of hundreds of cows and steers, lying as the
buffalo once had on the same land. Scotty's cowboys came back
to work, and together they searched out the herd and counted.

Scotty had lost eighty percent of his herd. The few survivors
were pitiful and feeble, worth little more than the dead animals.

When the count was finished Scotty went back to Fort Pierre.

"I can't pay anything on my loan now," he told the banker.
"My herd was almost wiped out."

"I know, I know," the banker said wearily. "It's the same story
for all the ranchers. You may as well just forget the loan, Mr.
Philip. The bank is going to have to write off all those cattle
loans—simply because no one will be able to pay. Ranching is
finished in Dakota."

"Now, wait a minute," Scotty said angrily. "I didn't ask you to
write off that loan. I don't want you to write it off. My name is on
that paper!"

The man looked at him curiously. "You mean you intend to
pay and to go on raising cattle here?"

"Yes. It'll take more than one bad winter to stop me. As a matter of fact, I'd like to borrow some more money to build my herd
up again."

The banker stared at Scotty and broke out laughing. "We
might just take another chance on you, Philip. Anyone with that
kind of nerve deserves it."

At least there was plentiful water in the summer of 1887.
Creeks and rivers ran full of melted snow water, and the grass
flourished. Scotty brought more cattle up from Texas and began
to rebuild his herd.

He sold a few head in the fall, enough to pay something on his
debts; fortunately, the winter was not severe and most of the herd

survived. In the early spring, he and two or three cowboys who had come to help him were out looking for newborn calves.

One March morning Scotty, alone, spotted a cow with a new calf in a sheltered, brushy area near the Bad River. The cow mooed pitifully; it was that sound that first led Scotty to the area. He was still a hundred yards away when he saw a huge white wolf prowling around the helpless calf.

Scotty had not brought a rifle. He drew his pistol and rode at full speed toward the animals. But before he got within range, he saw a lariat snake out of the bushes and settle in a loop around the wolf's neck. It was jerked tight, and the wolf leaped into the air like a puppet on a string.

A man on horseback came crashing into the open, dragging the wolf over the rocky ground until it was dead. The cowboy was a tall, muscular black man wearing dusty jeans and a red shirt.

"Good roping," Scotty called to him. "You saved my calf. I'm Scotty Philip."

The black cowboy rode close and looked at Scotty gravely. "Bunk White. I'm repping for Bill Benoist. You sure that's your calf? I thought I saw a W B Bar on that cow."

Scotty looked at the cow and saw that it was, indeed, Benoist's. The main job of cowboys who went out "repping" was to find strays mixed in with other herds. Bunk White had done good work this time.

"You're right," Scotty said. "She came a long way to have that calf, didn't she?"

"And now I've got to get both of 'em back. I'll just get that wolf untangled from my rope . . ."

"You're handy with that rope. If you're ever looking for another job, come and see me."

White gave Scotty another long, impassive look. "Might do that," he said. As he drove the cow and calf away down the riverbank, Scotty told himself to remember the name Bunk White.

The more cattle Scotty bought, the more skilled cowhands he needed to manage them. He would find a good man in Texas or Dakota, and then after a season or two the man would move on to some other place, some different work. Scotty always got along well with his men, but when they left in the fall he never knew how many would decide to come back the next spring.

He used some Indians, but most of the Dakota men still resisted the idea of any kind of steady "job." Some had their own cattle and did well raising them. Scotty knew, however, that the wild, free life of the past was still too close for the Dakotas to be satisfied as hired men.

When rations were distributed at the agency, Scotty and Sally were often invited to a feast given by one of her relatives. Ration day was like the day of a big buffalo kill in the old times. There was plenty, so everyone ate and celebrated. If there was not enough left over to last until the next ration day, then everyone would be hungry together—later.

Scotty noticed the rations becoming scantier and of poorer quality as the months passed. The food, which was supposed to replace wild game and was furnished by Uncle Sam, usually consisted of tough, stringy beef, pickled pork, grainy flour, cheap green coffee beans and brown sugar. The children became sickly and dull-eyed. Scotty brought gifts of vegetables and other foods when he came to visit, but these things were divided so quickly that they never went far.

Sally was more practical. She had a large, thriving garden, and she began interesting the Indian women she knew in growing vegetables. Sometimes she loaded the wagon with seeds, vegetables, and her children, and went visiting. When she came back, only the children were with her.

Dakota Territory was agitating for statehood that summer of

1888. As a Democrat, Scotty was increasingly in the minority. Supporters of Benjamin Harrison seemed to be everywhere, and when Harrison was elected President in the fall the Republicans became even more dominant in Dakota.

Harrison appointed a new head of the Indian Office in Washington: J. T. Morgan, a man who knew little about Indians and was influenced greatly by the views of eastern "experts." Changes began to move rapidly after that.

One spring evening Scotty's front door swung open without warning, and three Dakota men walked in. The children stared at the visitors, but without fear; they were used to unexpected company. Sally served coffee and warm fried bread. Then she took the children off to bed. The new baby, Clara, wailed for a few minutes and then the house was silent.

Scotty talked casually with the men, waiting for them to come to the point—for he sensed that this was no social call. Two of the men, Running Deer and Big Wolf, were old friends of Scotty's. The third, a Miniconjou holy man named Kicking Bear, sat silent through most of the talk. He was a tall man with a hard, lean body and deep-lined face. There was no friendliness or warmth in the looks he directed at Scotty.

"What is this 'Dawes Act' of which we have heard?" Running Deer asked finally. "Why is Crook coming to ask us to sign?"

Scotty hesitated as they watched him. He had read the newspaper accounts of the passage of the Dawes Act. He had also read the editorials hailing the new legislation as the "emancipation" of the American Indians. He was convinced that the whole thing was a mistake, or worse. But he knew what most of his neighbors would think of a white man who tried to influence Indians to resist.

"The Dawes Act is a new law," he began. "It is supposed to break up the reservation land into small farms. Every Dakota man is to receive a piece of land, two cows, a yoke of oxen, some tools, some seeds, and twenty dollars in cash. More money will be put aside for schooling for the children, and there will be cattle sent . . ."

"What if we want to live together with our relatives and the rest of the tribe, as we always have?" Big Wolf asked. "Why do they want us to live on farms like the *wasichus?*"

"What if the rains do not come, and our crops dry up again?" Running Deer asked.

Kicking Bear stood up, brushing aside the questions of the other two. He stared at Scotty contemptuously and asked in a soft, tight voice: "How much of our land are they taking this time?"

Scotty looked away from Kicking Bear's bright eyes. "Nine million acres. It's called 'surplus' land—after the farms are allotted. It will be sold and the money is to be used for the tribe . . ."

"Money!" Kicking Bear snarled the word. "They will take our land and give us more pieces of paper. Only it will not be so easy this time. Not . . . this . . . time!"

13

Ghost Scotty could sense fear, suspicion and mistrust ev-
Dance erywhere. As he talked with the Indians and other
whites on the reservation he heard few good words for the Land
Agreement they had all been brought in to sign. Yet General
Crook and his commission calmly continued joining in the feasts,
watching the dancing, and talking—always talking.

It was July, 1889. The Crook Land Commission had come to
the Cheyenne River Agency to get signatures of a majority of the
male Dakotas on the new Land Agreement set out in the Dawes
Act. There were some five hundred men camped around the
agency, listening to the speeches and talking among themselves.

Thus far, the commission had met with an almost united oppo-
sition to the land sale. At the other agencies they had at least had
the help of white men and mixed bloods in persuading the Indians
to sign, but here Scotty and most of his friends were as strongly
against the agreement as the fullbloods. Part of the reason was
that the boundary of the new Cheyenne River reservation was
being set so far to the north.

"The land is terrible up there," Scotty told the General when
he tried to persuade Scotty to sign. "There's no water at all. Here
these people in Washington are trying to get the Indians to start
farming, and then they want to move them up to an area that will

hardly support cattle! If the border were farther south, so they could use the good land around the Cheyenne River . . ."

"I see what you mean," Crook said. "It probably would be better. Of course, these boundaries were set up in Washington. I don't have the power to change anything in this document. But maybe after we get the signatures I could try to get them to move that border."

"You know they're not going to do it. The land speculators and settlers want that river land. General Crook, most of the Indians consider you a friend, or at least one of the best of the army officers. You've always tried to be fair with them. Why are you pushing this agreement now?"

Crook looked tired and discouraged. "They're going to have to give up the land, Philip. This agreement at least offers them a fair price for it. If they don't sign, they may end up losing the land with no return at all." He turned abruptly and walked away.

Scotty thought of Crook's words as the formal council began inside the main agency building. The General let the various Indians who wanted to speak have their say, and the long, rambling speeches went on for hours. The theme of their words was that the white man had taken enough. They also complained about the complexities of the agreement. The talk about acres, principal and interest, meant little to them. They could not understand boundary lines that could not be seen, or the time limits on buying the surplus land.

One elderly chief shook his head slowly and said, "There is nothing on a foundation at all. Everything is just wobbling. Even you yourselves don't know the price we are going to get for anything."

And it was true. There might be a rush of homesteaders into the newly opened lands, or perhaps a few wealthy cattlemen would buy it up, or maybe the land would not sell as quickly as white speculators thought. The only certain thing was that the Indians' reservations would shrink and shrink.

General Crook stood up late in the afternoon. He was still an impressive figure, with his broad shoulders and full beard and his deep-set eyes. "My friends," he said casually, "the agreement is on the table. If some of you are ready to sign it, come forward now."

Immediately a group of white "squawmen" and mixed bloods moved forward. Some of them were Scotty's neighbors on the Bad River. He was not sure what had made them decide to sign—most of them were farmers, and possibly they wanted more whites to move into the area. Or perhaps they wanted to buy the land themselves.

At first the room was deadly quiet. Scotty could see all eyes following the group. A muttering began, then angry shouting. Across the room Scotty saw Chief Hump, one of the fiercest of the Miniconjou Dakotas, raise his arm.

Two painted warriors, brandishing clubs, leaped through a window behind Hump and made for the table, yelling. One of them looked like Kicking Bear, though Scotty could not be sure. Others pushed forward. All the resentment and frustration of the past twenty years seemed to be boiling up. Scotty tried to talk to the men around him, urging them to keep things from getting out of hand, but they were in no mood to listen.

Crook stood in front of the table, quiet but immovable. Scotty had to admire his courage. Beside him, not quite so calm, were the agent and Major Randall of Fort Bennett. A few of the Indian police stood up with them, then a few more of the Dakotas.

Hump's warriors faced the General, shouting angrily. But they did not lay hands on him. Crook was respected. Besides, he was a very important man. To harm him would be to bring total disaster down on the tribe, and they knew that.

Crook said something to the interpreter, who had to shout to be heard above the din:

"General Crook says if there is any more trouble he will call the troops from Fort Bennett." The fort was only a short distance away; Scotty could see it through the window.

Gradually, the shouting became a mutter as the first men signed the Land Agreement. The council ended when the small group of men were through putting their names on the paper. Scotty went home to his ranch, more troubled than ever.

A few days later Scotty heard that Crook had left the Cheyenne River agency, and Agent McChesney was supposed to get the rest of the signatures needed for ratification. He got them. In fact, within a few weeks even Chief Hump had signed. It was the same story on the other reservations; the Dakotas were talked to, persuaded with promises and threats, pressured, confused, and finally enough names were put on the paper to make it law.

The land Scotty was living on might be considered "surplus" Indian land and be up for sale when the territory was thrown open for settlement. He would have to decide, if a buyer appeared, whether he wanted to stay where he was and purchase the land himself or relocate. He liked the Bad River area in many ways, but it was a long way from the cattle markets on the Missouri River. He began to investigate land for sale or lease in Stanley County, near the old trading post at Fort Pierre.

In August he took Sally and the children down to Pine Ridge for a visit with Zoe and Cornie Utterback. He would be too busy in the next few months for this kind of travel, and it had been a long time since Sally had seen the rest of her family. And they had never seen the youngest Philip child, George, Scotty's first son.

Cornie was still working as a teamster at Pine Ridge. He had a cabin on the edge of the agency. Scotty was amazed at the way the little community had changed since his last trip through: there was a boarding school for Indian children; a large council room; several office buildings; houses for the agent, interpreters and other employees; a large water tower, and storage buildings. Red Cloud had a large, two-story frame house which the government had built for him—it was even more impressive than the agent's house. But Scotty had heard that no furniture had been provided to go with the house, and the chief and his wives did not like "camping" in it, so that most of the time it stood empty.

As he drove his wagon through Pine Ridge, Scotty thought he noticed an unusual stirring about. Many Dakotas were gathered in small groups, talking rapidly. They did not look happy. Many people were moving about among the tepees near the agency.

"I wonder what's going on," Scotty said. "I can't remember ever seeing this place in such a stew . . ."

"Maybe there's been a fight or something." Posey, who was twelve now and almost full-grown, was always looking for excitement.

"Here comes Cornie, he can tell us," said Sally, shifting the baby from one arm to the other.

Cornie Utterback came striding toward them from the direction of the stables. He, too, looked worried and grim. When Scotty asked him what had happened, he climbed up to the wagon seat and spoke in a low voice.

"The Indian Affairs Office, in all its wisdom, has just announced that it is cutting rations at Pine Ridge by a million pounds."

"*Cutting* rations? But they hardly have enough to eat now!"

"Exactly. And, of course, it's the timing of the cut that is so beautiful. Less than a month after the good, obedient Dakotas sign away more of their land, the Great White Father cuts their rations. I'll tell you, people here who didn't sign that agreement

are really furious with the ones who did." Cornie dropped the
subject abruptly. "Well, why don't we stop here and let Sally and
the children walk on over to the cabin. Zoe's anxious to see them.
You and I can go and stable the horses, Scotty."

Scotty helped the little ones down and unhitched the horses.
As soon as Sally and the others were out of earshot, Cornie
moved close to Scotty.

"I didn't want to scare the children," he said, "but there's more
to this than just the ration cut. I think these people have had all
they can stand. They're angry, and desperate too. Something's
going to happen. You listen around here, there's all kinds of wild
rumors going around."

They took the horses to the stable and rubbed them down,
then began strolling back toward Cornie's house. It was late afternoon and cloudy enough to be almost dark. As they walked along
in the shadows of the big storehouse, they heard voices speaking
in rapid Dakota somewhere close by. Cornie put a hand on
Scotty's arm, and they stopped to listen.

The men must have been just around the corner, because most
of their words came through quite clearly in spite of the swift and
soft speech they used. Scotty's fluency in the language had im-
proved so much that he could understand perfectly.

"I tell you, God has come to earth again!" one voice said. "He
has appeared to the Crows—the same savior who was on earth
once before, the one the missionaries tell of."

"But he was a white man," someone protested.

"Now he has come back to earth as an Indian," the first voice
went on. "God was grieved by what the whites did to him, and
by what they have done to us. Men have seen him, in a place far
away to the south."

"What can a savior do for us now?" another man asked bitterly.

"He will bring back the buffalo," the speaker went on. "He will give us back the land. The dead will rise again, and we will see them."

"How can we know if this is true?" someone asked.

"We will send some of our trusted men to see this new messiah, and decide whether he can do what is promised. I am ready to go, and so are Good Thunder, Yellow Breast, Flat Iron and some others. We will find out the truth."

The voices stopped suddenly, and the two white men just had time to begin walking again before one of the Dakotas came around the corner and stopped, face to face with Scotty.

It was Kicking Bear, the holy man who had been to Scotty's ranch that spring.

He gave no greeting to Scotty, though he must have known who he was. Kicking Bear stared at the two whites silently, his full mouth turned down almost in a sneer of pure disgust. Then he moved gracefully away without a backward glance. Scotty felt his muscles relax, and realized that the Indian's stare had struck him like a blow.

"Must have been him doing the talking," Cornie said. "He's a leader, and a hater. What do you think of this talk about an Indian messiah?"

"I don't know. Maybe it's just a rumor. Maybe it'll die out by itself." Scotty wished he could feel more confidence in what he was saying. The whole incident had shaken him more than he wanted to admit.

They spent a week at Pine Ridge. Scotty watched Sally chattering happily with her Indian relatives and wondered whether she had ever regretted the marriage which set her apart. Zoe was in the same position, of course, but both of them seemed more natural somehow, more alive with their Dakota kin than with the white acquaintances of their husbands. Once, it had not seemed to matter so much. Now even the Dakotas themselves were being driven apart, suspecting each other, some willing to compromise with the white man and some stubbornly clinging to the old ways.

Some of the Dakotas around Pine Ridge were as unfriendly to Scotty as Kicking Bear had been; they watched him with undisguised hatred. Even men he had known for years and counted as friends were cool to him. Conversations stopped when he approached. He was not sorry when the time came to start back to the ranch.

Scotty's full energies were used up during the following months in a losing battle against a drought that was as powerful in its way as the winter blizzards. Creeks and waterholes dried up, even the tough prairie grass withered and the cattle were lean and hungry. Scotty's world was shrouded in dust. His ears, eyes and the creases in his face were full of dust. Dust gritted in his teeth. He and his cowhands rode miles through dust, driving the thirsty cattle to distant watering places.

In recent years Scotty had built up a crew of steady and skillful cowboys who worked for him through the spring, summer and fall. Among them were some of his old friends. Hi Kelly and Ike Humphrey, who had joined him in the Black Hills gold rush, showed up one April and went to work for him. And on a buying trip to Texas he ran into Tom Beverly, the man who had guided him on his first and only buffalo hunt. Tom had come back to South Dakota as Scotty's foreman. Bunk White, the black cowboy Scotty had met years before, rode in to ask for a job and was hired to "rep."

But no amount of help could fatten a herd of cattle in the kind of weather South Dakota had in that summer of 1889. And in even worse shape than the cattlemen were the farmers, whose crops dried up and burned in the sun.

The Indians who had been supplementing their meager rations with garden vegetables now had to depend on the rations alone—and they had been cut. There was little feasting, though the Dakotas still shared what they had.

In the fall Scotty sold off most of his cattle, thin and stringy as they were. He could not afford to be wiped out in another bad winter; he was still trying to clear up his debts from the last one.

Then winter came, not with the heavy snows of the previous year but with something just as bad. Sickness made the rounds of the already weakened and hungry people of western South Dakota. Measles and flu brought death to family after family. Scotty and Sally attended more than one Indian burial feast, and the feasts were pitifully scanty.

George, the eight-month-old baby, came down with whooping cough in the first real cold snap. Night after night the family was kept awake by his coughing and wheezing. Sally tried everything: patent medicine, Indian herb cures, ointments and chest rubs. Scotty made a trip to the agency and talked to the doctor, but he was told that there was nothing more to be done, that the disease would have to run its course. George died before Christmas.

The pattern of grief was familiar this time, but no less painful. Scotty had dreamed of the future of this first son, and had loved the baby with the affection he felt for all his children. It was agonizing to put the tiny body in a box in the frozen ground and watch the snow drift over the lonely grave.

Nearly every Indian family Scotty knew lost at least one child that winter. But the sense of shared grief and sympathy was not as strong as it had been when Mary had died. Scotty tried to help his Dakota neighbors, many of whom were on the edge of starvation. They were courteous to him, but their faces were closed and they did not trust him.

Scotty could not blame them. Ten years before, he had imagined that the Indians and whites in Dakota would gradually grow
into one people, with mutual respect and a shared future. He had
even hoped to be some kind of bridge between the two cultures.
Instead, he was an outsider, helplessly watching as the extremes
on both sides grew farther and farther apart.

To the Indians, he knew, the *wasichus* were now permanent
enemies who had broken all their promises and were trying to
starve the Dakotas into submission while stealing their land. The
whites could not understand why the Indians had not made more
"progress," had not become more like them. Ignorant of or indifferent to the poverty in which the Indians lived, whites saw
them as lazy or stupid.

And Scotty stood between, unable to change the direction in
which things were moving.

Conditions did not improve very much with the end of winter,
though the epidemics finally disappeared. Congress, busy with
"more important measures," did not get around to restoring the
cut in rations for the Dakota tribes. Gardens failed again in another drought as bad as the one of the previous summer. The reservation land was officially opened for sale, but by this time the
bad weather had discouraged most of the potential buyers.

Scotty struggled through another summer and decided it would
be his last one on the Bad River. The grazing land was not capable of supporting the number of cattle Scotty wanted to run, especially with the lack of rainfall drying up the grasses. He began
negotiating a deal for some property in Stanley County along the
Missouri River.

The fall roundup was harder than usual, for Scotty's cattle had
wandered far in search of food and water. The riders would have
to scatter for miles to find them all.

The morning they started out, Sally walked out to help Scotty
pack his bedroll, rope, and gun on the strong back of the stallion

he liked to ride. The rising sun glowed orange like a prairie fire in the distance.

"You riding north?" Sally asked.

"Some of us'll have to, why?"

"I heard some people are dancing on Cherry Creek. Be careful."

Scotty studied his wife's face. She was not a worrier, but today it was tight and her dark eyes shadowed. "Dancing?" he asked her. "You mean this new religion? I'd like to see that. What makes you say I should be careful?"

"Kicking Bear, Hump, Yellow Thigh and some of the others there—this isn't just a religion to them. It's a chance for revenge."

Sally added nothing more to her warning. This was one of those times when the Indian side of her personality was very strong, and Scotty felt curiously separated from her, as though she had a secret knowledge that he could never fathom.

The first few days of the roundup were very busy, as Scotty and his men located the bulk of the "L-7" cattle not too far from the ranch. After dark each night the men shared a hot meal by the chuck wagon, rolled up in their blankets and slept on the ground.

Bunk White came back from a "repping" trip to the west with a dozen more of Scotty's cattle, but still there were at least thirty animals unaccounted for after the first part of the roundup was over. So Scotty left two men with the main herd and scattered out the rest of the riders to search for the missing cattle. He, himself, rode north toward Cherry Creek.

Scotty tried to pretend that it was just a business trip, that he was only looking for stray cattle. But he wanted to see the dancing, too. Whites in Dakota were referring to the new craze as the "Ghost Dance," because it was supposed to call forth the ghosts of long-dead animals and people.

Scotty rode out to see the ghost dancers' camp on Cherry Creek.

The ghost dancing had been going on at all the reservations for months. A delegation of Dakotas had visited the founder of the new religion, a Piute Indian named Wovoka whom many believed to be the messiah. Those who had seen Wovoka returned to spread stories of his magical power and to teach the Dakotas the dance which had been given to Wovoka by God.

Disciples of the religion believed that a new world was about to be created, one in which the Indian race would live with dignity and power. They would enjoy eternal life, and there would be abundant game and plenty to eat for all. The buffalo would come back. Some believed that all this was ordained to take place in the spring of 1891.

Scotty had heard a great deal about the messiah religion, but he had never seen the ghost dance being performed. Some whites claimed it was a kind of war dance intended to stir up hatred and create trouble. Settlers in western Dakota were more than a little nervous about the whole business.

From a ridge overlooking Cherry Creek, Scotty saw the ghost dance camp the second day after he started out. There were some tepees, a great many horses tethered together and a moving crowd of people gathered around some kind of pole. He tied his horse to a tree near the bank of the creek and approached on foot.

When he got closer, Scotty saw that the pole was a sapling with an American flag fluttering from the top of it. Perhaps a hundred people were dancing around the pole, their hands clasped and their feet shuffling. Women and children danced along with the men. A man stood in the middle, near the pole, leading the singing. His face was painted and he had an eagle feather in his hair, as did most of the other men. Scotty recognized him as Kicking Bear.

Other people were ranged around the outside of the circle, watching, and Scotty joined them quietly. Kicking Bear was

singing, the other dancers repeating his song after him. Scotty listened carefully and got the words:

> The buffalo are coming, the buffalo are coming
> The Crow has brought the message to the tribe;
> The father says so, the father says so.
> The buffalo are walking,
> Over the whole earth they are walking.
> The people are coming home,
> The people are coming home,
> Says my father, says my father.

The dancers moved faster and faster. Some leaped into the air,
shouting. Others fell to the ground and lay rigid as the dance
swept around them.

Scotty turned to a young Dakota who stood near him to ask a
question. The man looked vaguely familiar, but Scotty could not
place him.

"Why are they lying on the ground?" Scotty asked in Dakota.

"They are visiting the spirit world. When they wake they'll
tell about their visions." The young man paused, then looked
Scotty in the eye and added in perfect English: "You'd better not
stay around here too long, white man."

14

Wounded Knee

"Don't I know you? My name is Scotty Philip . . ." Scotty studied the young Dakota, trying to remember where he had seen him before.

"Yes, you know me. Plenty Horses. You helped send me off to Carlisle when I was a boy." The man's precise English made an odd contrast with his appearance: long hair, blanket and moccasins, Indian-style leggings.

"Plenty Horses! Of course—but that must have been ten years ago. I didn't help send you away. I just left you at my house, asleep, and when I came back you were gone."

"I always thought you told the police where to find me." Plenty Horses shrugged, his handsome face twisted with bitterness. "It doesn't matter. Now I'm an educated Indian, a Carlisle graduate, come back to lead my people. Only I don't know where to lead them, and they don't want to be led."

"With your education . . ."

"Mr. Philip, with my education I'm no longer an Indian, but I'm not a white man either. I don't want to *be* a white man. Well, things may change now." He turned his brooding gaze toward the ghost dancers again and smiled faintly. "Maybe they're right, and the messiah will come next spring."

"Surely you can't believe all that. It's so fantastic!"

"Fantastic? No more fantastic than the white man's religion that was drilled into me at Carlisle. The dance is based on Christianity, you know. Your Bible says that Jesus will come again, and after what your people did to him the first time—why shouldn't he come as an Indian?"

Plenty Horses turned suddenly and moved away into the crowd. Scotty was left with the music of the ghost dance in his ears and the vision of the Indian messiah in his mind.

The Dakotas Scotty knew were much more religious than whites. They saw a spiritual dimension to everything they did, every experience they had, and they never shut their religion off from the rest of their lives. He realized now that the dance was more than a fanatical cult; it was an expression of their desperate faith. At the same time he felt sure that the new faith was misdirected and would lead to disappointment, perhaps even disaster. Thinking of these things, he started to walk away.

The people watched him impassively. There was not one friendly greeting, even from men with whom Scotty had worked or shared a feast. No one threatened him, but there was none of the usual courtesy and kindness the Dakotas showed to visitors. He was an outsider, and not a welcome guest.

Scotty found six of his cattle in a draw at the southern end of the Cheyenne River reservation, not far from Cherry Creek. He also found the carcasses of four more animals, recently killed and butchered. He could not blame the Indians for killing cattle to feed their starving families. But he was beginning to worry about their increasing boldness and hostility. They had not even bothered to cover up their tracks.

After the roundup Scotty wrote an angry letter to Commissioner of Indian Affairs Morgan, urging him to restore the cut in the Dakotas' beef ration. Morgan wrote back that this could only be done by a special act of Congress. Democrat Scotty had no influential connections with the Republican administrations of President Harrison or South Dakota's Governor Mellette, but he wrote more letters anyway.

Scotty was running nearly a thousand head of cattle, and he paid little notice to the few that disappeared. Some of his neighbors were more concerned. They urged him to join in asking the state government for troops and weapons to crush the potential "uprising" before it got out of hand.

"Don't you count on being safe because your wife's an Indian," one rancher told him. "Some of those fullbloods hate the half-breeds and anybody else who won't go along with the ghost dance. You'd better think of your family if you won't think of your cattle."

As the man rode away, Scotty thought about what he had said. It was true that the Dakotas themselves were being pulled apart by the messiah cult. Those who did not join the dancing were shunned by those who did. The old atmosphere of trust that Scotty remembered among the Indian people was gone. Still, he believed that bringing in troops would be more likely to cause trouble than to stop it. Surely the whole thing would die out in the spring, when people realized that the miracle had not happened.

In November he traveled to Stanley County and spent two weeks getting a house built on the land he intended to buy. He had decided to hang onto the Bad River land as well, if he could, and run cattle on both places. But he felt sure that the new home, three miles north of Fort Pierre, near the new town of Stanley, would be a less isolated place for Sally and the children. Too, it would be easier for him to ship cattle in and out with the rail connections at the river available for transportation.

He got back to the old ranch in mid-November, to find a dozen young Brules camped on his place. Sally told him that a man named Yellow Thigh seemed to be their leader, and that they had been at the ranch all day. She had given them some food at noon, but still they made no sign of preparing to leave. Scotty walked out to talk with them.

It was cold, though there was no snow on the ground yet. The men were camped around an open fire with their horses tethered nearby. They were wrapped in blankets. Scotty could see that under the blankets they were wearing "ghost shirts" made of cotton or flour sacks and marked with magical signs such as circles, crescents, and symbols of the eagle, crow and buffalo. Each man had a Winchester rifle close beside him.

Scotty greeted them in Dakota, being as friendly as he could at the beginning. They replied with grunts and harsh laughter when he asked if he could help them.

"What do you want here, then?" he asked, growing angry.

"We camp where we please," Yellow Thigh answered, with a rudeness that was completely out of character for a Dakota. The others watched with great interest, and the stocky Brule licked his lips and went on. "I've killed *wasichus* before. And I'll do it again. You, Philip, are raising horses for my people to ride and cattle for us to eat."

"You be off by morning," Scotty growled in a strangled voice. He walked slowly away, deliberately exposing his broad back to the rifles.

He could not sleep that night. Scotty had never been afraid of Indians; not since his first growing-up year in the West. But he was afraid now. He did not fear what the fanatics of the ghost dance might do to him so much as he worried about the safety of his family and the danger of a bloody confrontation that would destroy whites and Dakotas alike.

The holy men were saying that "ghost shirts," such as those worn by Yellow Thigh and his men, could not be penetrated by

white men's bullets. Reckless and angry men who believed they
could not be killed might do almost anything.

The Brules were gone the next morning, but Scotty could not
forget about them. He wrote out a telegram to send to Governor
Mellette, describing what he had seen and heard, and urging the
state to take some action. Then he read it to Sally.

"Will the soldiers come?" she asked.

"I don't know. Maybe."

She looked away, and Scotty thought he could see in her face a
memory of the bloody yard of Fort Robinson. When the soldiers
came, death came too . . . No, he told himself, not this time.
Something has to be done to keep the extremists from taking
over, to *prevent* bloodshed.

He sent the telegram.

A month later, with Sally and the children moved to the new
Stanley County house, Scotty was back at Pine Ridge helping
Cornie Utterback move frightened Indians and whites from
outlying districts to the agency.

Sitting Bull had been killed. News of the famous old chief's
death at the hands of Indian police who had tried to arrest him
caused a new hysteria throughout western Dakota. The ghost
dance leaders were angrier and more determined than ever. In
the middle were many wavering, bewildered people, equally
wary of the soldiers and the dancers.

Scotty and Cornie helped guide wagonloads of women and
children into the agency. Not far from Pine Ridge was a tent-city
housing more than a thousand of General Brooke's soldiers.
Other troops and an eager South Dakota militia were out patrol-
ling the area. They were particularly anxious to capture Big Foot
and his large band of Miniconjou Dakotas, now hiding somewhere in the Badlands.

Scotty went back to spend Christmas with his family, but he

was uneasy the whole time. His foreboding was not helped by reading the local papers. Most of them urged the army and militia to immediately make "good Indians" of the ghost dancers (assuming their readers would agree that "the only good Indian is a dead Indian").

On December 29, Scotty took a wagon into Fort Pierre to get some lumber he needed and food supplies for Sally. In the grocery store an excited discussion was going on between the clerk and two customers. When Scotty walked in the clerk called to him:

"Say, Mr. Philip, did you know those redskins finally surrendered? Telegram just came through this morning! The army's got 'em surrounded at some creek east of the Badlands—it's got a funny name, sore knee or something . . ."

"Wounded Knee Creek?" Scotty asked.

"Yep, that's it. They're gonna bring 'em in to Pine Ridge as soon as they take the weapons away."

"Why bring 'em in?" one of the customers asked. He was a thin, bony man with ginger-colored hair. "Seems to me they ought to get rid of the whole bunch of trouble-makers right now. We've been coddling these savages too long as it is."

"You're right," agreed a plump, pink-faced man with a beard, who looked vaguely like the pictures of Santa Claus. "It's time this state was made safe for decent white families. I heard those ghost dancers have thousands of dollars worth of stolen cattle with them, and they've kidnapped some white women and killed more than one family of ranchers . . ."

"Do you have the names of these people?" Scotty asked.

"Names?" The pink-faced man hesitated. "No, but I hear what's going on."

"The only killing I know about is Sitting Bull, and of course he was on the other side." Scotty observed the irritated looks the others gave him. None of them had ever met his wife, they knew him only as a big cattle-raiser who had recently moved into Stanley County.

"Mister, you sound like one of these Eastern injun-lovers," the clerk said.

"I just don't believe in shooting down women and children, and that's what would happen if a fight started out there. Those men have their families along, and a lot of innocent people who just ran because they were afraid. There are only a few real trouble-makers with Big Foot. Even Kicking Bear and his band have already given themselves up . . ."

Scotty saw from the men's faces that they were not interested in thinking of Indians as individuals. He paid for his supplies in the midst of a cold silence and left.

All the way home he thought about the situation around Pine Ridge. The soldiers, the refugees, the suspicious and angry Indians—it was not a combination that would make for an easy settlement.

By the time he arrived at the ranch, he had decided to ride back to Pine Ridge. "Even if there's no trouble," he explained to Sally, "Cornie will have to help all those people get home. Some of them will be hungry, and there isn't that much extra food around Pine Ridge in the middle of the winter."

"When will you come back?" she asked.

"In a week or so. You'll be all right?"

Scotty felt a pang as she nodded. Sally had to manage alone more often than he sometimes realized. She had another new baby to look after, Stanley, a healthy boy but a worry nevertheless after the loss of two other babies in infancy. Amy, Tina and Olive were old enough to be of some help around the house, but Sally still had a tremendous amount of work to do every day. She did it without complaining, seemingly with pleasure, and her love of the family filled her mind and her world.

He stopped overnight at the Bad River ranch, checking on the cattle there and the cowboys who were looking after them for him. Then he rode south.

Scotty knew there was trouble before he got to Pine Ridge. He started out early in the morning on December 30, 1890. When he approached White Clay Creek, fifteen miles northwest of Pine Ridge, he heard the noise of many voices, drums and occasional shots. The day was bitter cold, with a ground blizzard sweeping and swirling over the prairie. Scotty rode cautiously around the well-worn trail. The noise became louder, and he knew a large group of Indians must be camped near the creek. He circled around the place, listening. Singing pierced the cold air, and the songs were of death and mourning.

It was after dark when Scotty made it to Pine Ridge, stiff with cold. He went straight to Cornie's cabin. Zoe opened the door for him.

She stared at him with surprise for a moment. "Scotty—what brought you back?" she asked.

"I heard about Big Foot's band being captured, thought maybe I could help get people resettled. What's happened?"

Zoe took his snowy coat and hat and motioned him to a chair by the stove. She sank down wearily across from him. "Someone started shooting when the soldiers were trying to take their guns. We don't know just how it happened. There was a fight. We could hear that big Hotchkiss gun booming all yesterday afternoon. Then the soldiers came back with their dead and wounded, I guess thirty men or so. And they brought some Indians. But there are more back at Wounded Knee—nobody knows how many were killed or hurt."

"What did Red Cloud, Kicking Bear and all the others do when they heard about it?"

"Most of them left the agency. I don't know where they are or what they'll do. When they heard what happened . . ."

Scotty nodded. "Fort Robinson all over again. Dear God,

couldn't we have settled something just once without all this kill-ing?" He stared at the glowing door of the stove, listening to the fire hiss and pop. "Where's Cornie?"

"Over at the chapel, helping Reverend Cook tear out the pews and fix it up for a hospital. He should be back soon to get some sleep. Tomorrow they're going out to Wounded Knee to see if there's anyone left alive there. The army won't let anyone go to-night; they want to be sure everything's quiet first."

Cornie came home late and was too tired to do much talking. He still did not know the extent of the casualties or the facts as to how the fight had started.

They tried to get some rest before dawn, but Scotty could not sleep. He listened to the wind whining around the corner of the cabin, gusting occasionally through a crack and across his face.

Once, in a kind of half-sleep, his mind drifted back to child-hood and the stories an ancient uncle had told him. In his imagi-nation he saw the kilted highlanders marching off to battle, strid-ing bravely, bagpipes howling, on their way to Culloden Moor to fight for Bonnie Prince Charlie. They faced the English, and were cut to pieces by the newly-invented British guns. He saw them dying on the moor or escaping to the highlands only to live as fugitives.

The echo of the bagpipes was still in his mind when he heard Cornie stoking up the fire at first light.

It was a grim procession that rode back to Wounded Knee. With Cornie and Scotty were Charles Eastman, the Indian doc-tor who worked at Pine Ridge, some other white civilians, and a few of the Indians who had not fled the agency.

They saw the first body almost three miles from Wounded Knee Creek. It was a woman, shot in the head and frozen.

"Look," said Dr. Eastman, "the way she has the shawl pulled over her face. As if she didn't want to see . . ."

They rode on, following a deep ravine that led toward the

creek. At first there was no sound but the wind and the squeaking of the wagon that had been brought to transport the wounded—if any were found. As they came upon more bodies, those of children and old people, all caught in the attempt to run away, the Dakotas from Pine Ridge began the songs of mourning. Their singing and moaning made Scotty shiver and reminded him again of bagpipes with their minor key, unearthly notes.

At the site of the camp the bodies were heaped together like firewood. The party found a few women and children still alive, but no men.

The trip back to Pine Ridge was even worse than the ride out. A baby not more than a year old slept on Eastman's shoulder. Along the ridge beyond the creek, some Indian horsemen watched. Scotty wanted to be sick, to weep, to ease somehow the tightness in his chest. He joined the singing.

15

Rattlesnake Hill Scotty could not bring himself to go back with the burial party the next day. By that time more whites had gathered at Pine Ridge. Some of them were eager to see the famous "battlefield," and perhaps bring back a ghost shirt as a souvenir. Later he heard how the bodies had all been gathered up and dumped into a common grave at the top of the hill where the Hotchkiss cannon had been.

Once Scotty went to the Episcopal chapel at the agency, which was now a hospital for the wounded. Zoe was there, patiently changing bandages and trying to sooth the injured children. Scotty counted four Indian men, and thirty-four women and children in the improvised hospital. Dr. Eastman was doing his best to help them, and working beside him, Scotty was surprised to see V. A. McGillycuddy, former superintendent of the Pine Ridge agency. He remembered, now, that McGillycuddy had been an army surgeon at one time.

"I didn't know you were back at Pine Ridge," Scotty said when he had a chance to speak to McGillycuddy.

"Haven't been here long—thought I could help. Terrible thing . . ." McGillycuddy's voice trailed off. His shoulders sagged wearily; he had none of his old military self-assurance. "Maybe I could have kept this from happening, if I'd been here," he added bitterly. He had lost his post through a political change six years before. Scotty had never liked McGillycuddy particularly, but he thought the man might have been better able to cope with the ghost dancers than the weak, frightened agent now at Pine Ridge if . . .

If. Scotty had been trying for three days to avoid asking himself if his telegram had contributed to the hysteria that ended at Wounded Knee. He was not so influential that one telegram from him would bring action from the government. Others had been much more insistent in calling for troops. Still, he looked at the wounded Indians and wondered why, in spite of his good will, he always found himself a helpless bystander when trouble came. "It's not easy to be in the middle," Long Joe Larribee had told him once.

Greens were hung along the walls of the little chapel, and in one corner still stood a lovely, blasphemous Christmas tree.

By January 7 the Dakotas were beginning to drift back to the agency, and it looked as though the bloodshed was over. Scotty had to get back home; he had already been gone longer than he had intended. Since there were still many angry Indian men roaming the countryside, he was told by the soldiers not to attempt to ride cross-country alone. So he decided to board the train at Rushville, Nebraska, and go by rail to the Missouri River, where he could take another train to Pierre.

As he and Cornie started out for Rushville, they noticed a stir in the army camp on the edge of the agency. Cornie stopped one of the 9th Cavalry "buffalo soldiers" (as the black soldiers were called by the Indians) and asked him what had happened.

"Another killing," the man said. "Officer named Casey shot in cold blood by some Sioux. Plenty Horses, I think they call him."

Scotty read the story later, in the newspapers he bought in

Pierre. Plenty Horses had shot and killed Lt. Edward Casey in the White Clay Valley as the officer and another soldier rode toward the Dakota camp to try to negotiate a peaceful return to the agency.

The young Dakota was tried for murder in Deadwood that March, and was freed on the grounds that he had killed Casey during a "state of war." It was a statement attributed to Plenty Horses during the trial that stuck in Scotty's mind:

> I am an Indian. Five years I attended Carlisle and was educated in the ways of the white man. I was lonely. I shot the lieutenant so I might make a place for myself among my people.

History books called it the Battle of Wounded Knee, and the whole event was recorded as the last armed confrontation between United States troops and Indians. Certainly this fight and its aftermath crushed forever any hope of the Indian people that they might bring back their old life as it had been. Many years later holy man Black Elk told John Neihardt:

> I did not know then how much was ended. When I look back now from this high hill of my old age, I can still see the butchered women and children lying heaped and scattered all along the crooked gulch as plain as when I saw them with eyes still young. And I can see that something else died there in the bloody mud, and was buried in the blizzard. A people's dream died there. It was a beautiful dream.[1]

The pain of Wounded Knee did not fade quickly. Rations were finally increased. Broken families struggled to hold themselves together; orphans were adopted by distant relatives and even the most fanatical gave up the ghost dance.

In the years that followed, Scotty tried to mend his friendships

[1] John Neihardt, *Black Elk Speaks*, University of Nebraska Press, Lincoln, 1961.

with the Indian people. He was able to help some of the young men get started as ranchers, and he and Sally still took part in the round of visiting that was so much a part of the Dakota culture. But as Scotty's business interests increased, he had less time for the leisurely social life that Sally enjoyed. Convinced that the future of western South Dakota lay in the production of beef cattle, he went on building his herds.

During that summer of 1891 he hired a steamboat to transport ten loads of Minnesota cattle across the river to his pastureland in Stanley County. He increased the number of cowboys working for him each year, and he did more and more traveling to negotiate purchases and sales.

Sally stayed home. Involved in raising the children, she was not interested in making trips any longer than an occasional visit to her sister's place. When he returned from a business trip, Scotty always sensed again the strength of her gentleness and warmth in the very walls.

He was gone when Tina died of a sudden and vicious infection. As soon as Sally got word to him, he came home, but somehow she had taken care of everything and had held things together, as she always did. Scotty grieved for his ten-year-old daughter even more deeply than he had for the two infants they had lost. There had been more time to know her, there were more memories.

Five children remained to fill the house with their shouts and tears, and in 1895 Stanley got the brother he had longed for, Roderick. Another girl, Annie, was born in 1897. Scotty watched them all growing tall and strong, with shining dark hair and ruddy complexions. They looked neither like Indians nor like Spanish-Scottish-whites but were an attractive combination of the two.

In 1896 Scotty was approached by a Minnesota man named Charles Steube, with the idea of forming a large cattle outfit. Scotty would get steers from the East and would fatten them on the Dakota grassland; it would be a much larger operation than one man could run on his own. So the Minnesota and Dakota Cattle Company was formed, with Scotty, Steube and a New Ulm banker as partners. It was known, from the brand they adopted, as the "73 Outfit." Scotty continued to buy some cattle under his own L-7 brand, but his work as manager of the 73 Outfit took most of his time. He had to keep track of thousands of cattle, a large herd of horses and dozens of cowboys.

He had little time for correspondence that was not related to business, but he did hear occasionally from his family in Kansas and Scotland. During the summer of 1897 he learned that his nephew, another George Philip, the son of his favorite brother Robert, had come to the United States. The boy was in poor health and had gone to work on Alex's Kansas ranch. Then, a few weeks later, Scotty heard that young George had disappeared and was in Colorado somewhere.

Scotty smiled to himself, remembering his own departure from Kansas and his first months in Nebraska and Dakota. He wrote to his older brother George:

"To George—I understand Bob's boy is roaming somewhere through the West. If you know where he is, tell him to come up here and I will put him to work."

Later Scotty had a note from his nephew, saying he would be coming to Pierre on the train. Scotty met him at the railroad station in the middle of the night. Even in the dark he thought the boy looked like a Philip: dark, strong-featured and sturdy.

"You look healthy enough," Scotty commented as he swung the boy's bags into the buckboard. "I thought you came to the

United States because you had lung fever or something."

George looked up at Scotty uneasily. "I'm a lot better."

"Never knew TB cleared up that fast."

As they rode toward the ranch George was quiet, staring at the sweep of the stars across the open darkness. Scotty knew how this country looked to people who saw it for the first time, especially at night. It was like being taken back to the beginning of the world, when nothing existed but earth and sky. Kansas could look that way too, but there was a different, wilder taste to the South Dakota air.

"I might as well tell you the truth to begin with, Uncle James," George said suddenly. "I never had lung fever. I just pretended to have it so I could come to America. Everyone kept saying the American plains were so dry and healthy—anyway, I was apprenticed to a marine engineer. Five years, I was supposed to work for him. I hated it. So I got this cough, and that gave me the idea."

"You've got some rascal in you, just like the rest of us. And why did you leave Alex in the middle of the summer?"

"We didn't get along. All he's interested in is that farm. So I just packed up and left one night. And that's another thing, Uncle James, I don't know how long I'll be staying here. I mean, I'm not going to promise to work for you all year or anything. I don't like to be tied down like that."

"You're stubborn as I am, young George. We'll get along. If we don't, you can leave any time."

"If you don't have room for me to stay with you, I can get a place somewhere. Your wife might not appreciate another member of the family, and I've got a big appetite—in spite of my TB." George grinned in the moonlight, and Scotty found himself liking the young man more all the time.

"Sally will be glad to have you. With her people, you know,

'family' is a lot bigger than the way we think of it. Aunts and uncles, grandparents, cousins, nieces and nephews are as close as brothers and sisters. She'll be mothering you the minute you walk in."

Scotty's prediction proved correct. George's own mother had died ten years before, and he soon regarded Sally as his second mother. The children liked his gaiety and his stories. Posey, almost the same age as George, helped him learn the work of a Dakota cowboy. The summer passed quickly, and there was no talk of George moving on.

In September Scotty took George and Posey with him to the Bad River ranch to help with the roundup. By now George had the look of an old hand. He wore his dusty work pants, cotton shirt and vest with an easy air; his boots no longer looked new, and his hat was cocked at an angle over his tanned face. It was only when he spoke that his Scottish burr betrayed him as a newcomer.

Riding beside him, Posey was lean, copper-skinned and totally at home on the land. Scotty enjoyed watching them work together.

They rode down toward the Badlands, following the trail of a large group of strays. It was hot for September. Gnats and mosquitoes buzzed around their ears, and the dust dried out their throats.

"I'll climb that hill, see if I can spot them," George said. He dismounted and ran up a small, rocky mound to look.

Scotty watched him go. Just as he reached the top of the hill, something moved a few yards away. Scotty squinted against the sun, then saw what it was and sucked in his breath.

"George!" he called. "Behind you—don't move!"

George turned and saw it: a huge mass of rattlesnakes, twined around each other like a skein of living yarn.

This was not the first time Scotty had seen rattlesnakes "ball up." They did it every fall, preparing to hibernate in the rocks through the winter. Now other snakes were coming out of the cracks on the hill, disturbed by George's passing. Their rattles whirred warningly. If George panicked, he would be dead.

"Get your quirt," Scotty called. "We'll start clearing a path from down here, and you work your way down slow. Watch where you step, and don't hurry!"

The three of them untied the quirts (rawhide whips) they always had on their wrists. George stood very still for a moment, looking down, and then he flicked the quirt with an expert motion and killed the snake a few feet from his boots. Posey and Scotty began at the bottom of the hill, not trying to get all the rattlers but only those in George's way.

Scotty soon noticed a sickening stink, expanded by the heat of the sun. He had killed many snakes before, but never so many in one place. By the time George reached them and they hurried him down off the hill, the smell was overpowering.

George never wavered until he was down and away from the place. Then he sat down very suddenly, turned his head and was sick. Scotty felt close to throwing up, himself, and he saw that Posey was sweating profusely.

"I'll never know how we got off there without one of us being bit," Scotty said in a choked voice. "We'd better camp over by the creekbed and rest awhile."

Posey and Scotty recovered after a short time, but George was sick all day. They found the cattle about a mile farther along the trail, and somehow got them headed back toward the place where the roundup wagon was located. George rode mechanically, slumped in his saddle. They got the strayed animals back to camp at sunset, but still George could not touch any of the hot grub that the cook had saved for them. Scotty found him sitting cross-legged on the ground, looking as weak as a city-bred girl.

"Wishing you'd never left old Scotland?" Scotty asked gently. George shook his head and sat a little straighter. "It's just the smell—made me sick. You know, when I first came out here I was a little bit afraid of rattlesnakes. But after today, well, *one* won't seem like anything."

Scotty smiled and nodded. He was sorry his brother could not have seen the young man who had grown up in this long South Dakota summer. From that time on George was one of Scotty's most valuable men—and also more and more like one of his own children.

Each year the 73 Outfit grew bigger, and its financial affairs became more complicated. And each summer there was more friction between Scotty and his partners. For one thing, Scotty did his bookkeeping in his head. He was good at figures and saw no reason to spell them out in endless ledgers. Everyone in the cattle business knew Scotty, and they knew he was an honest man. Even Eastern bankers would give him large loans on his signature alone. But Steube and Mullen kept badgering him for reports, estimates, paper work.

In the summer of 1899 they had it out on the banks of the Missouri at Fort Pierre as a large shipment of cattle was being docked. Scotty called a banker friend the same morning and arranged to sell his interest in the Minnesota and Dakota Cattle Company.

It was a relief to be on his own again. The weather was good, and there was enough rain to fatten the cattle he brought in each year. Scotty Philip was becoming a wealthy man. He made investments, and they prospered as the cattle did. He dabbled in politics, served as a county commissioner and later as a state senator.

Scotty now left most of the hard riding and cattle herding to his cowboys. He was busy with buying and selling, and, much as he disliked it, correspondence.

One morning late in 1900 he found a letter from Washington, D.C., among the notes from business acquaintances and banks. He opened it curiously, trying to think who might be writing to him from the capitol. The letter, typed on crisp white paper, read:

Dear Mr. Philip.

Perhaps you remember the man you rescued from the mud near your ranch some fourteen years ago. You very kindly let me spend the night at your home, and we talked about the danger of the extinction of the American bison.

That danger is more acute now than it was then. The number of bison left in this country cannot be more than a few hundred.

I am now the director of the New York Zoological Park, but I've come to Washington to try to persuade the Congress to pass a law protecting the bison. It would be most helpful if you would write to your congressman and urge him to support this measure.

Within the next few years the fate of the American bison will be decided, by nature or by man.

Most cordially yours,
William T. Hornaday

Scotty answered the letter immediately, somewhat ashamed that an eastern taxidermist had to lead the fight to preserve an animal of the western plains. He wrote to his congressman, too, supporting Hornaday's proposed law. Then he forgot the buffalo, for a while.

His memory was jogged again when he visited the spring roundup on the Bad River. The day he arrived some cowboys from several northern outfits were exchanging news with his own men. From them he heard the news that Pete Dupree had died.

One of the hands from the Dupree outfit was a Frenchman named Paul Clogenson, called "Pollyvoo" most of the time.

Scotty remembered hearing that Pollyvoo had special charge of Dupree's buffalo during the winters.

"What's going to happen to Pete's buffalo, now that he's gone?" Scotty asked him.

Pollyvoo raised his eyebrows and began rolling a cigarette. "I think they'll be sold. Most of Pete's relatives thought he was crazy to keep them this long."

"How many are there?"

"About eighty now."

"Are they hard to keep?"

Pollyvoo laughed. "Those devils make tending cattle seem like raising kittens. Takes three or four men to handle one bull buffalo. They gore the horses, break down fences and it's almost impossible to rope 'em. On top of all that you have to protect the calves from wolves, and then trying to *brand* them . . ."

Something about the way he spoke made Scotty say, "But you like working with them, don't you?"

The man looked at him, squinting his eyes and scowling. "One of those monsters will probably kill me some day if they aren't sold. But I guess I do like it. It's a contest, see, and I don't think many men could take on even one buffalo. Besides, they're like those old beasts I used to read about in storybooks. Big, wild, and terrible."

"How did Pete keep them separated from the cattle?"

"He didn't." Pollyvoo took paper and loose tobacco from a pocket and began rolling a cigarette. "So now along with the buffalo we got cattalo. Most worthless animal you ever saw; cross them with beef cattle and you get freaks. I'd say if the buffalo ain't killed for meat or the hides, they'll be gone anyway unless they're fenced off and raised alone. Well, they'll all be up for sale soon."

"Who do you think might buy them?"

"Probably somebody who wants to butcher them and have a big party so he can get his name in the newspapers for a day or two."

The rest of the men from the Dupree outfit were getting ready to ride away, and Pollyvoo tightened his saddle and mounted his horse.

"Who's the administrator of Dupree's estate?" Scotty called after him.

"Doug Carlin."

Scotty thought about it through the rest of the roundup. He knew Doug Carlin, Dupree's brother-in-law. Doug was a good man, but too busy with his own ranching interests to be very concerned with taking on the care of eighty buffalo.

There were only a few hundred American bison left in the country they had once dominated, so Hornaday said. In ten years or less, they would probably be gone.

But what real difference did it make? Wild buffalo could never again roam the plains by the hundreds of thousands. They could not roam at will anywhere; there was no room for them. And they were not animals that would take to life in a zoo. The buffalo could never again exist in numbers great enough to serve any practical purpose. Once they had fed, clothed, sheltered a whole people, and even held a place in their religion. That day was over.

16

Buffalo Scotty thought about Dupree's buffalo. When he
Pasture got home after the roundup, he tried to put them
out of his mind, but without success.

Still, cattle were his business, and cattle absorbed most of his
time and thought. That spring of 1901 he received a large shipment of eastern cattle to be fattened on his range through the
summer. He and a good-sized crew went to the Missouri River
landing at the little town of Evarts to look the new animals over
and bring them back to the ranch. They found the ferryboat se-
curely tied to the dock on the west side of the river, and the cattle
milling and bawling on the east side.

"Can't ferry 'em for you, Mr. Philip," the owner of the boat
apologized. "Smith's tried everything, but he just can't get the
engine going right. Maybe tomorrow . . ."

"Not tomorrow, I want those cattle over here *now!*" Scotty
knew he was being unreasonable. It seemed harder to be patient
or even polite as he grew older. Still, the idea of spending the
night in Evarts was more than he could bear. "We'll just have to
swim them over," he decided.

The river was relatively narrow and shallow at Evarts, but it
was never an easy task to swim cattle through the treacherous
Missouri. Scotty had done it frequently in the old days. Now the

prospect of plunging into "Old Muddy" on horseback made him throw one last, angry glance at the ferryman tinkering with the boat's engine, as though the delay were his fault. He looked like a new employee—Smith, the owner had called him. Probably he had been careless and scraped over a sandbar or something.

"Move out," Scotty called, and he and his cowboys spurred their horses off the bank and into the cold, murky water.

It was easy enough going across. They all had good, sure-footed horses, and there were only a few spots with strong undertow. But when they reached the other side and drove the young Herefords into the water, the struggle to get them safely across absorbed every ounce of Scotty's strength. He yelled until he was hoarse, trying to keep the frightened animals heading for the other bank and out of danger. Broken tree branches and other debris came swirling by. His legs grew numb with the cold, though the spring sun still warmed his face.

He had almost reached the ferryboat and the shore when a calf turned in the strong current and started floating downstream, its head bobbing up and down. Scotty leaned as far as he could and reached for the calf. He grasped it by the neck, struggled to turn it—and slid off his horse.

He was under water before he fully realized what had happened. Reaching for the surface, he felt as though his clothes were made of concrete. Finally, he got his head out, gasped, and as his own horse slammed into him, he went under again.

Then someone had him by one arm. He was hauled partly out of the water; another pair of hands grasped his other arm, and he found himself dripping all over the deck of the ferryboat.

"You all right?" a bearded man asked. "Swallow much water?"

Scotty started to speak, choked and tried again. "Not more'n a couple of gallons," he sputtered. "My horse . . ."

"He's all right." The owner of the ferryboat was standing beside the bearded stranger. "One of your men brought him in. The cattle are all up, too, so just relax. One of your men is getting some dry clothes for you."

Scotty looked back at the other man, the ferryman "Smith." There was something familiar about him. If it were not for the beard, Scotty was sure he would remember. The man seemed to be studying him just as intently.

"Scotty?" the ferryman said slowly. "Why, I thought those Indians took care of you twenty-five years ago! I'm Boston Smith!"

They had dinner together at the local restaurant, after Scotty had changed clothes and counted the cattle. Through the meal they talked of many things, but the conversation kept going back to that time in the Black Hills when they had last seen each other.

"I went straight to Billings, never even looked back," Boston laughed. "I was so scared . . . Why, for years after that I expected to see that shaggy scalp of yours on some buck's belt."

"And I was sure they caught you!" said Scotty.

"Guess we were both pretty lucky. In those days, them Sioux had things their own way out there. Well, that's all changed now. The army took care of 'em. And I got my share—I was with Crook for a while, you know."

Boston rambled on, telling stories of his Indian-fighting days. Watching him, Scotty drifted back mentally. He was seventeen again, huddled above an Indian village with Boston Smith. His skin tingled with fear and excitement. The savages below were his enemies.

"I say, you got a family?" Boston broke into Scotty's dreaming.

"What? Oh, sure. My wife Sally, and eight children. Come by and meet them some day." Scotty smiled to himself, wondering what Smith would think of his Indian wife.

Riding home that night, Scotty thought about how close he and Boston Smith had been once, and how they had barely recognized each other today. The changes were more than physical. It was strange to realize how even memory could not bridge the gap between what he was now and what he had been.

One night shortly after he got home he brought out the best buggy, hitched a team of horses and told Sally he wanted her to go for a ride with him. The children were curious; the younger ones teased to go along, and the older ones made remarks about Scotty becoming romantic in his "old age." He ignored them all and drove away with Sally beside him.

He took her to the banks of the Missouri. A three-quarter moon bathed the "Big Muddy" in golden light. Along both banks, the strange rounded hills crouched like overgrown buffalo. There were no houses in sight, though a distant artificial glow marked the twin towns of Fort Pierre and Pierre.

Sally did not ask why he had brought her there. He supposed she had lived with him long enough to know he would speak when he was ready. Or maybe it was her instinctive Indian way of waiting for the proper time to talk of important things.

"I'd thought to get more cattle to run in this pasture," Scotty began. "There are more than three thousand acres available along the river here. But now I've got another idea."

"Pete Dupree's buffalo?"

"How did you know?" Scotty stared at his wife, amazed.

"I heard Pete had died. And George told me you'd mentioned something about his buffalo, that you wondered what would happen to them."

"Pete was letting them breed with cattle, producing those worthless cattalo. That's got to stop. I'd have to fence the whole pasture. And not with ordinary fencing, either. It would take a crew of men to take care of them, and there'd be no profit in it. What do you think?"

Sally was silent, looking out over the empty land. When she finally answered him, she spoke in such a low voice he could hardly hear her.

"It will be very bad for my people if the day ever comes when there are no more buffalo on the earth. Some of them still believe that, when the time comes, the Dakotas will die too. Even if they cannot hunt buffalo any more, it would help to know some of them are alive. But you, Scotty, why do you want to do this?"

Scotty had not been sure of his reasons until the moment he put them into words for Sally. "I don't think I'd be doing any great thing by saving a few buffalo," he said. "I can't make time go backward or change the things that have happened in the last twenty years. But I can't watch them destroyed. It's too easy to judge everything by the way it fits into our world, our business. The buffalo have a right to live."

"You're a good man—for a *wasichu*." She smiled impishly at him, and he knew they had agreed.

It took weeks to fence the huge pasture. The posts had to be more than six feet high and strong enough to withstand the power of a charging buffalo. Heavy woven wire and barbed wire were wound around the posts to the very top. The cowboys could not go chasing wild buffalo all over western South Dakota; the herd would have to stay within the enclosure or it could not be kept.

The "buffalo pasture," as everyone was beginning to call it, was large enough to give the animals plenty of freedom within the fences. There was good grass, water and shelter from winter storms in the breaks and draws. The majestic Missouri rolled down one side of the pasture, but the banks were high enough to protect against floods.

When word of Scotty's plan got out, he was teased repeatedly by the many who thought he was out of his mind to take on such a project.

"Going to train them to pull a carriage, are you Scotty?"

"I hear they're calling this place 'Philip's Folly.' "

"How soon you going to get a saddle on one of those critters?"

"Ever try to milk a buffalo cow?"

Scotty laughed as good-naturedly as he could, or ignored the jibes. He did not try to explain his idea to anyone but Sally. Those who were capable of understanding would understand— without words. He did not care what the others thought.

By late summer, 1901, the buffalo pasture was ready. Scotty went up to the Dupree place on the Cheyenne River reservation to get his buffalo. George, Bunk White and four other cowhands went along. Carlin, the administrator of the Dupree estate, had agreed to send some of his men to help to get the buffalo to Scotty's ranch. Pollyvoo was one of them. He and the other Dupree men already had the buffalo bunched together in a little valley when Scotty and the others arrived.

They reined up their horses on a hill, looking down at the milling, snorting animals below. The species might be nearly extinct, but there was nothing dead or dying about these buffalo. They were powerful, wild and dangerous.

"We're going to drive them to the pasture like cattle?" George asked in a small voice.

17

An Act of When the first fifty-seven buffalo came up
Congress the creekbed toward his ranch, Scotty was
waiting and watching. He had not gone along on the drive; he
seldom did these days. It took an exceptionally strong horse to
carry his more than two hundred pounds for very long. And at
the age of forty-three, he no longer enjoyed sleeping on the
ground and spending days in the saddle. So after settling the deal
with Doug Carlin he had come on home to wait for his men to
bring the animals.

He stood by a cottonwood tree not far from the buffalo pasture
fence. It was so hot the air was shimmering. He heard them coming before he saw the distant cloud of dust moving toward the
pasture. Fifty-seven buffalo could make quite a noise with their
hooves and their snorting. He tried to imagine the old days, when
a hundred thousand of them might have run by this spot in one
herd.

Some of his white-faced cattle were grazing nearby, and Scotty
saw them watching as the buffalo came into view. Cattle simply
could not register amazement by expression, but he thought he
could sense at least puzzlement in the way they looked at the
newcomers. They could not know that they had replaced these
others, who had once shared the western grazing land with the
Indians.

Bunk, George and the others looked tense and exhausted. Their faces were shiny with sweat and streaked with dirt. They rode warily around the buffalo, not driving them all but working to keep a few "lead" bulls going in the right direction. The gates to the pasture were open wide, but as the buffalo came close they began to shy away from the strong fence.

"Get one of those leaders through," Scotty yelled.

Bunk and George rode up on either side of a shaggy bull at the front of the herd. For a moment Scotty was afraid that the bull would charge one of them; it pawed the ground nervously and swung its massive head from side to side. Pollyvoo came shouting from behind, then, and the bull ran on through the gate. The others followed, urged by the cowboys; at last the gate creaked shut and Scotty fastened its strong lock.

"Whew," Bunk said, climbing down out of the saddle. "I believe I'd rather herd a thousand spooky cows in a thunderstorm."

"They give you much trouble on the way?" Scotty asked.

"Oh, not much," George said sarcastically. "Only that none of us got five minutes of sleep, and we wasted half a day chasing a renegade bull that didn't want to come along, and then there were the wolves . . ."

"We got 'em here, anyhow," Bunk laughed. "Don't know if we could have done it if it hadn't been for old Pollyvoo. He sure does know buffalo."

Scotty turned to the Frenchman, who was taking a long drink from his water flask. "We could use some help keeping these animals," he said. "You going back to the Dupree outfit, or do you want to work for me—as sort of a 'buffalo foreman'?"

Pollyvoo wiped his mouth and stared through the fence at the buffalo, squinting his eyes in a strange way he had. "Filthy hard work," he said. "But I'm used to it. All right."

By fall they had eighty-three head of buffalo behind the fence. Pollyvoo and his helpers watched them carefully, and they seemed to thrive. Scotty was too busy to think about them or look at them very often. He had to earn his living with cattle and tend to his other investments.

That was the last summer George Philip was on the ranch. He went off to college in the fall, with the ambitions of becoming a lawyer. Scotty missed him, and he missed the other children, who were at boarding school, and Annie, who died suddenly after a fall in 1902. The house seemed strangely quiet during the long evenings.

Occasionally, when he had an hour or two to spare, Scotty liked to ride out to the buffalo pasture and watch the big animals. It was good to know that they were safe from hunters inside the fence. It was not always easy to keep them in the pasture. In the winter, when the snowbanks piled high, Pollyvoo had all he could handle to prevent the buffalo from climbing over the drifts and out. The cowboys grumbled at having to shovel down great banks of snow in order to keep the buffalo in, but it had to be done. And the fence had to be repaired constantly, a time-consuming job.

The herd multiplied as the years went on. By 1904 there were nearly three hundred animals in the buffalo pasture. They were becoming famous; tourists came out to the pasture from Pierre to look at the unusual beasts. Some of them even drove out in the new motor-cars that were a novelty in the cities.

One spring afternoon Scotty was looking over some of the new buffalo calves with Pollyvoo when a chugging, hiccoughing noise announced the approach of an automobile. Buffalo and horses alike shied at the sound, and Scotty strolled back to the gate to see who was coming.

A fat, balding man in a hot-looking duster stopped his car—an "Olds-mobile"—and got out. He peered through the fence, ignoring Scotty and Pollyvoo.

"At last," he said in a squeaky voice. "I've been driving for hours, looking for these ugly creatures." He turned to Scotty, who was wearing his wide-brimmed Stetson hat and dusty work clothes. "You, can you tell me where to find the owner of these animals?"

Scotty stared down at him until the man began to twitch nervously, and then said "Why?"

"Well, I want to buy some of them."

"Why?" Scotty asked again.

"I'd like to talk to the owner," the little man said stiffly.

"He's the owner." Pollyvoo grinned and jerked a thumb in Scotty's direction.

"Oh, I see. Mr. Philip, is it? My name is Draper, and I represent a client who'd like to buy some of these bison."

"Why?" Scotty said for the third time.

Draper looked exasperated. He spoke loudly and slowly, as though he thought Scotty were slightly deaf or perhaps mentally incompetent. "My client is having a dinner in Omaha next week. It's for a large group of business associates, important people. He wants to serve something different, you see, to impress them. We'd heard about these bison you have up here, so he sent me up to order a carload or two, to be shipped by train. If you can tell me how much prime meat we'd get off each of these . . ."

"No," said Scotty.

"What?"

"I'm not selling a carload of buffalo to be butchered for a dinner in Omaha."

"Name your price."

"I said no!"

Finally convinced, Draper got back into his automobile and drove away, looking angry and shocked at the same time.

It was not the first time Scotty had been approached by men who wanted buffalo meat. As the animals became more and more rare, people began to think of them as a delicacy, or at least a novelty.

Scotty leaned against the gatepost, watching his buffalo. They would be safe enough while he lived. But they were expensive to keep, and the three thousand acres in his buffalo pasture might be in demand for other uses. Homesteaders were moving into western South Dakota, trying to farm the dry ground and plowing up the rich grasses. The towns and cities were growing. He was leasing this land from the federal government, but the day might come when some official decided it should be used for something more productive than the preservation of buffalo.

A few months later Scotty made a business trip to Oklahoma. He bought some cattle and equipment, hired several new hands and then took a day to travel to Pawnee.

Scotty had kept in touch with Hornaday through the past few years and had followed the work of the new American Bison Society. He knew that the only buffalo left in the United States, besides Scotty's own herd, were owned by Charles Jones of Kansas, Charles Goodnight of the famous Goodnight Ranch in Texas and Major Gordon W. Lillie of Pawnee.

Lillie was a well-known rancher, and Scotty had met him several times on buying trips. Lately Scotty had heard that Major Lillie was trying to get Congress to set aside land for a buffalo preserve in Oklahoma.

"It has to be done," Major Lillie told Scotty as they shared lunch at the hotel in Pawnee. "Individuals like you and me can't protect the American bison forever. We have to have laws, and special parks . . ."

"But will the Congress care enough to do it?" Scotty asked. "I know William Hornaday's been trying for years to get protective laws passed, and he hasn't had much success."

"I think they will, now. President Roosevelt is concerned, and

I think he'll use his influence to help. I'm going to Washington next year when Congressman McGuire introduces a bill to establish the buffalo preserve near Fort Sill, and I'll do what I can to get votes for it."

"We should have something like that in South Dakota," Scotty said thoughtfully.

On a blustery winter morning in 1906, Scotty prepared to leave for Washington. In his pocket was a copy of the proposed bill which would set aside thirty-five hundred acres of land on the west bank of the Missouri River "exclusively for the pasturing of native buffalo and for no other purpose."

The whole Philip family had come to the station to see him off. Scotty looked at them, lined up on the platform, and suddenly wished he had words to tell them what they meant to him. Amy, Olive, Hazel and Clara were grown women. Beautiful and poised, they were all graduates of an excellent boarding school. Scotty had never cared for formal education, but he had insisted that his children finish their schooling. They would have to make their way in the modern world, and without education that would be very difficult.

Scotty's two half-grown sons, Stanley and Rod, were still in school. But they had also worked around the ranch almost from the time they could walk and were home now on vacation. They looked sturdy and capable, standing on either side of their mother.

Sally smiled her goodbye. She was growing older, but the marks of age did not make her face hard or sharp. It had been more than twenty-five years since their marriage, but Scotty still saw in her the girl from Long Joe Larribee's store.

"Goodbye," he said to all of them. "When I come back, I'm going to bring a guarantee from the United States Government

that there'll be buffalo around for a long time yet. At least I hope
I am."

Scotty sat in the balcony of the United States House of Representatives just a week later. He had been to Washington before
and had even visited the House and Senate, but never had he felt
so personally involved in the workings of government.

He looked down on the large room filled with men from all
over the country, each with a different background, different set
of beliefs, and a different goal in mind. It was a wonder they ever
got together on anything. Yet somehow, over the years, men like
these had achieved a sort of unity. They had made terrible mistakes—Scotty thought of the long series of decisions which had
nearly destroyed American Indians. In spite of all this, the country had survived and had made some progress toward achieving a
good and free life for all people.

The clerk was reading a new bill to be discussed, and Scotty
snapped to attention at the title:

"H.R. 13542; Leasing Lands in Stanley County, S. Dak., for a
Buffalo Pasture."

"Mr. Speaker, I ask unanimous consent for the consideration of
this bill." Burke of South Dakota, who had agreed to present the
bill for Scotty, was on his feet. "In Stanley County, South Dakota, there is a gentleman who has a herd of native buffalo. He
has them in a pasture on the Missouri River and he wants to get
additional land adjoining the pasture so as to enlarge it . . . This
bill simply authorizes the Secretary of the Interior to lease 3,500
acres of that land coming up to the township where these buffalo
are now pastured, and provides that it can be used for a buffalo
pasture, and for no other purpose."

It was strange to hear himself being discussed in the House of
Representatives. A few minor questions were asked and answered, and then a Mississippi Congressman got up to object. He

felt that the bill ought to provide for some rent to be paid for the use of the land. Scotty wanted to say that he'd be glad to pay rent, or buy the land if they'd let him. But it was in the public domain and technically open for homesteading. In almost twenty years no one had taken out a claim on the land, however, because it was so hilly and rough.

A Mr. Lacey of Iowa, whom Scotty knew to be one of the backers of Hornaday's conservation laws, entered the discussion.

"These buffalo are kept by Mr. Philip, who married an Indian wife," said Lacey. Scotty wondered briefly what that had to do with the discussion, but Lacey went on. "Instead of charging Mr. Philip anything, I think the Government could very well afford to give him some aid, direct aid, in his laudable purpose of saving these animals from extermination . . . This herd, which is the third largest in the country and perhaps the finest in its quality, should be saved. Instead of mixing the breed, as they have in other herds, Mr. Philip has continued to breed the pure plains buffalo; and he succeeded, and will go a long ways to preserve this magnificent animal from extinction."

The debate went on. Many of the congressmen walked in and out of the room casually; others listened with bored expressions. Scotty knew this was a very minor matter to most of them.

Finally it was agreed that rental for the land would be set at fifty dollars a year. This seemed to satisfy everyone.

Without more discussion, H.R. 13542 was passed. A few weeks later, on March 12, 1906, it also passed the Senate. President Theodore Roosevelt signed the bill into law, and Scotty went home.

18

The Buffalo Are Walking "Giddap!" Scotty yelled at his car, a new Overland, but the wheels kept spinning deeper and deeper in the mud. He turned the engine off and sat looking through the rain-streaked windshield. He would have to go for help, of course, but he hated the thought of getting out and walking a mile or more in the rain.

Scotty Philip was tired. He had been sick more in the last two years than at any time in his whole life. Now, in the summer of 1911, he felt as weak as an old man.

He had been driving back from Pierre to the ranch when the rainstorm caught him. He wished he had a carriage and team, or at least a good horse. The new automobiles were all right in good weather and on decent roads, but they were worthless in the gumbo around the Missouri River after a rain.

Wearily, he got out and began trudging toward the home of a rancher he knew nearby. He told himself that a South Dakotan should always be glad of rain. There was never too much moisture for the long grass, the thirsty animals and humans. One of Scotty's latest projects was an irrigation system he hoped to build around Pierre.

He wanted to do many things, but somehow he had a feeling that his time was running out. A few weeks before, he had suffered what the doctor called a mild stroke; as he recovered, he faced the fact that it could happen again at any time.

When he was on his feet again he supervised the building of a family burial plot near the buffalo pasture, on a bluff overlooking the Missouri. The work on that would be finished by tonight.

The rain dripped from the brim of his hat, and the wind blew it into his eyes. He shivered in his wet clothes. On his neighbor's porch, he stamped some of the mud from his boots and knocked on the door.

"What are you doing out on a day like this, Scotty?" the man asked.

"My Overland's stuck down there. Could you let me borrow a team to pull it out?"

"Sure. I'll come along to help. Let's hope we don't get a thunderstorm to spook the horses. Say, are you all right? Sure you don't want me to drive you home in the buckboard? We could get the car later . . ."

"No. I want to get that blasted thing out of the mud before these roads get any worse." Scotty resented the suggestion that he was some kind of weakling. All his life he had been bigger and stronger than other men; he was not ready now to become sickly or pampered.

As he pushed at the back of the car while the horses pulled the front, Scotty felt like Samson after his haircut. His muscles were flabby, and his whole body feeble and sore. When the car limped out of the mudhole Scotty almost fell in.

"Thanks for the help," he called to the owner of the horses.

"Anything for the Buffalo King," the man said, smiling.

Scotty waved and drove away. He was not comfortable with the title some newspaper reporter had conferred on him—"The Buffalo King"—but there seemed to be no use protesting it. His herd numbered more than three hundred now, and was said to be the largest and finest herd of purebred American bison in existence.

He drove up the road to the house, avoiding the ruts, and parked the car in the yard. Stepping out into the rain again, he pulled his jacket around him in a vain effort to warm himself. It was strange to be so cold in July.

Sally met him at the door, helped him get out of his wet clothes, brought him a clean shirt and settled him in an overstuffed chair by the stove.

"I'll build a fire to take the chill off the room," she said.

Watching her, Scotty felt a rush of gratitude. "How many times have you wrapped me up like this, after a blizzard or a rainstorm?"

She smiled and shrugged.

"Remember that time I fell in that pond, in the blizzard of '87? Didn't think I'd ever be warm again. Well, what have you been doing today?"

"Oh, some sewing, and working in the garden, things like that. An old man came by, walking along the river with his grandson. I gave them lunch. Red Arrow, the holy man—you remember him?"

Scotty nodded.

"Last night he saw a raven by the door of his house. So he came all the way up here today to take one last look at the buffalo. He brought his grandson along; they were on their way to the Buffalo Pasture."

"You really think he'll die tonight?" Scotty asked.

"He saw a raven." Sally had lived among whites for years and had watched her children grow up as educated, "modern" people, but Scotty knew the stream of Dakota faith ran deep in her. Scotty also realized the the old man probably would die. The Dakotas had an uncanny way of knowing and accepting the cycle of life and death; he wished that he could be as sure of his beliefs as they were of theirs.

"Look, they're just coming back now," Sally said from the window.

Scotty joined her there and watched the two walk slowly by, the old man partly supported by the straight-backed young Dakota. The rain had stopped, but footing was still treacherous. The boy was dressed in jeans and a plaid shirt, like any western South Dakota youngster. Yet there was something special in the look of them together, the mutual respect, the grace with which they went.

Lately some of the eastern newspapers had taken to referring to the Indian people as the "vanishing Americans." Scotty disliked the term, though it grew out of a well-intentioned concern. The Indians were not going to disappear in a puff of smoke. They were too strong for that.

Watching the boy and his grandfather, Scotty felt sure that the Dakota people would survive. And it would not be a mere physical survival, like that of the buffalo. Some day America might learn from their special knack for living in harmony with each other and with nature.

"One thing I do hope, Sally," he said as the old man and the boy disappeared into the distance. "I hope that I'll be remembered as a builder instead of a killer. Too many of us have come out here just to take what we could get."

Sally stared thoughtfully into the fire. "Things are different now. For my people, they are bad. Who can we blame? The soldiers, the settlers, the government? I don't know. But you're a good man, and you've tried."

At five o'clock the next morning, July 23, 1911, Scotty woke feeling violently ill. It was another brain hemorrhage. He was unconscious almost immediately, and he died two hours later.

On July 26 the funeral was held at the ranch house near the Buffalo Pasture. Newspaper accounts later called it "the largest gathering of its kind ever held in the Northwest."

A special train was dispatched by the Chicago and North Western Railway to bring hundreds of bankers, commissionmen, merchants and cattlemen to the funeral. All of Scotty's cowhands were there, and many others from nearby ranches who had worked for Scotty or had known him.

From the Cheyenne River and Pine Ridge reservations came Indian friends, most of them wearing their finest Dakota clothing and ornaments. Sally's relatives brought gifts, in the traditional way, to honor Scotty's memory.

After the service, conducted by the Episcopal minister at the house, the whole group went out to the cemetery for the burial. Hundreds of carriages and automobiles wound the two miles to the hill overlooking the Missouri. They were followed by others on horseback and even by a few people walking behind.

As the last words were pronounced by the minister and the coffin was being lowered into the grave, someone noticed movement on the other side of the buffalo fence. Soon all the people around the grave turned to look.

Outlined against the sky several hundred buffalo appeared in the nearby hills. They moved down along the fence, quietly, like belated mourners.

Sources

1. BOOKS

Andrist, Ralph K., *The Long Death*, Collier Books, New York, 1964.

Bordeaux, William J., *Custer's Conqueror*, Smith & Co., Sioux Falls, S.D., 1951(?).

Branch, E. Douglas, *The Hunting of the Buffalo*, University of Nebraska Press, Lincoln, 1962.

Eastman, Charles A., *From the Deep Woods to Civilization*, Little, Brown & Co., Boston, 1926.

Hall, Bert, *Roundup Years*, State Publishing Co., Pierre, S.D., 1956.

Hyde, George E., *A Sioux Chronicle*, University of Oklahoma Press, Norman, 1956.

Lee, Bob, and Williams, Dick, *The Last Grass Frontier*, Black Hills Publishers, Inc., Sturgis, S.D., 1964.

McGillycuddy, Julia, *McGillycuddy Agent*, Stanford University Press, Stanford, Cal., 1941.

Miller, Nyle H., *Kansas*, Kansas State Historical Society, Topeka, 1961.

Neihardt, John G., *Black Elk Speaks*, University of Nebraska Press, Lincoln, 1961.

Peattie, Roderick, ed., *The Black Hills*, Vanguard Press, New York, 1952.

Philip, George, *Scotty Philip*, South Dakota Historical Collections, Vol. XX, Hipple Printing Co., Pierre, S.D., 1940.

———, *Prairie Progress in West Central South Dakota*, Historical Society of Old Stanley County, Midwest Beach, Sioux Falls, S.D., 1968.

Reutter, Winifred, *Early Dakota Days,* Mellette County, White River, S.D., 1962.

Sandoz, Mari, *Cheyenne Autumn,* McGraw-Hill, N.Y., 1953.

———, *Crazy Horse,* University of Nebraska Press, Lincoln, 1942.

Utley, Robert M., *The Last Days of the Sioux Nation,* Yale University Press, New Haven, Conn., 1963.

2. PAMPHLETS AND GOVERNMENT REPORTS.

Densmore, Frances, "Teton Sioux Music," Bureau of American Ethnology, Bulletin 61, Washington, D.C., 1918.

Malan, Vernon D., and Schusky, Ernest L., "The Dakota Indian Community," Rural Sociology Department, South Dakota State University, Brookings, S.D., Bulletin No. 55.

———, "The Dakota Indian Religion," Rural Sociology Department, South Dakota State University, Brookings, S.D., 1959.

———, "The Social System of the Dakota Indians," Rural Sociology Department, South Dakota State University, Brookings, S.D., 1962.

Mooney, James, "The Ghost Dance Religion and the Sioux Outbreak of 1890," Annual Report of the United States Bureau of Ethnology, Vol. 14, 1892–93, Washington, D.C.

3. OTHER SOURCES.

Letters from George Philip to his daughter, Mrs. Jean Mitchell of Sturgis, S.D.

Information from the files on James "Scotty" Philip in the South Dakota Historical Society Museum, Pierre, S.D.

Interviews with Mrs. Jean Mitchell, Mrs. Stanley Philip, Mrs. Billy Ann Rheborg and Mrs. Flora Ziemann.